The eB yers Guide to the Galaxy

"The must have eBay marketing & advertising book for Buyers & Sellers"

By
Harry J. Misner
www.HarryMisner.com

Disclaimer

The Author makes no representations or warranties regarding the accuracy or completeness of the contents of this work. The advice, theories, and strategies listed in this book may NOT be suitable for all situations. Any use of this information in violation of any federal, state or local law is prohibited. All trademarks, trade names, services marks and logos referenced herein belong to their respective companies.

TABLE OF CONTENTS

TABLE OF CONTENTS II

PART 3

PART 4

Introduction

EBay began its operations in San Jose, California, in September 1995 with the pioneering work of Pierre Omidyar. EBay is the largest person-to-person and business to person marketplace. It uses the novel concept of online auction sales to enable and empower individuals (and businesses) around the world to sell almost all types of products and services.

EBay can make you stinking rich, because eBay is an opportunity of a lifetime, and you are literally days or even weeks away from making plenty of money on eBay. It is not a dream or a wish, but it is reality and it is very closer and more realistic than you think.

Thousands of people from all over the world are making lot of money on eBay. At any moment, millions of items and services are on sale. Billions of dollars' worth of property successfully passes through eBay, not merely every year, but every month and day.

EBay is an unusual e-commerce site because it does not actually sell or trade anything; it simply provides a viable mechanism through which other people can sell online.

Besides the relatively low-dollar individual sales of collectibles and "garage sale" items, many established merchants sell cars and real estate, computers and antiques, and electronics and jewelry. In addition, not just in the United States or Canada, either. EBay operates and provides an opportunity around the world, in Western Europe and— through an investment, MercadoLibre.com—in Latin America, Hong Kong, Malaysia, Australia, and India. It is a vast, international marketplace, in which millions of individuals and merchants sell millions of products and services.

Recently, other auction sites have also sprung up to compete with eBay. Yahoo!, Amazon.com, and others have all tried to try their lick to knock down the notable giant. Despite their inhuman efforts, eBay continues to dominate to have the lion's share of the market, although other auction sites, like Overstock and Yahoo! are still trying to enhance their market share. Selling or trading on eBay is not as hard or difficult as you think, because it is quite easy and simple. You can definitely do it and succeed! The associated risks are few; the opportunities are unlimited, while there is no office rent or employees to pay. EBay markets your product for you and this perhaps the biggest advantage with this site. Therefore, you do not need to worry about advertising or marketing.

EBay is a beautiful and cajoling thing! To make unlimited money through e Bay, you must learn, understand and apply what you learn. If you have any products or services to sell, eBay helps you find someone to buy them. It is all automated and streamlined; just fill out the online forms and eBay launches and runs the entire auction process for your benefit. When the auction is over, the highest bidder wins; after receiving payment from the bidder, the seller then ships the item, and with this, another auction is successfully completed.

You can do all the selling activities by using your own personal computer; collect the payments sent to you electronically with your bank or through the mail, and then dispatch the items you sell, via a courier agency. It is that simple, it is relatively very easy, and you do not need to make substantial investment. This little book gives you more than enough information and details to become the most successful seller on eBay and it provides you great tips and advice.

Importance of eBay

After you start buying and selling on e Bay, you will observe that there are plenty of options and choices. The following are the most important and beneficial ones:

- EBay is not only a great place carry out your business it's also a great site to make and meet like-minded friends and join a worldwide community.

- A positive advantage of an eBay business is that you can start the operation and later abandon without using lot of money. Just imagine that you own a business like a bakery or a hair salon or a barbershop or some kind of restaurant. How many businesses are you able to start and stop within a short time that without spending too much money? An eBay business can be turned on and off just like a light switch and still you may not be adversely affected. When you are ready to go back to your business, just start selling once again. That is quite flexibility one can have in business.

- For many people, saving money is the biggest and most notable benefit of all. You will spend less money on eBay than you will buy the same goods at a store (even with shipping costs), and sometimes there are huge bargains to gain and accumulate.

- Online auction sites attract a large amount of traffic thus making them an ideal place to make use of readily available and widespread exposure for your products and/or company. Because of the immense opportunity for buying highly valued and premium items at a relatively low price, the broad range of products and services available on the site, the ease of access to them and the social/economical benefits of the auction process, one can find a large number of bidders on e Bay;

- You can find all the products of your choice on eBay, with relative ease.

- One man's trash is another man's treasure. Next time, when you are cleaning out your attic or garage, never ever, throw away what you find there—there is probably something precious you have, that someone else wants desperately wishing to buy. It is so easy to make money on eBay, as you will note down throughout this book. It is so easy, in fact, that people have been able to make their living selling products and services through eBay.

- Looking or scouring for hard-to-find items, finding hidden treasures on eBay, outbidding others in an adrenaline pumping, fast-and-furious action—online auctions can be a great form of thrill, fun and relishing entertainment.

Getting Started

The first thing that you may need to do is to go sign up for eBay. There are some good courses and tutorials given right on eBay's Web site. They also have a number of online videos that will show you the basics of buying and selling. You can download them to learn the basics. You begin (as either a buyer or a seller) by registering your details with eBay. Registration is free, simple easy, and relatively quick.

EBay asks all members to provide a valid physical address and a telephone number. They do not disclose this information to any third parties outside the eBay site, although they will supply appropriate personal data to other eBay users, especially sellers, on their special request.

You can get more details from eBay's Privacy Policy, found at

at:pages.ebay.com/help/policies/privacy-policy.html.

You can register as an eBay user by following these steps:

Click the "register now" button or, from the eBay home page, click the Register link above the Navigation Bar.

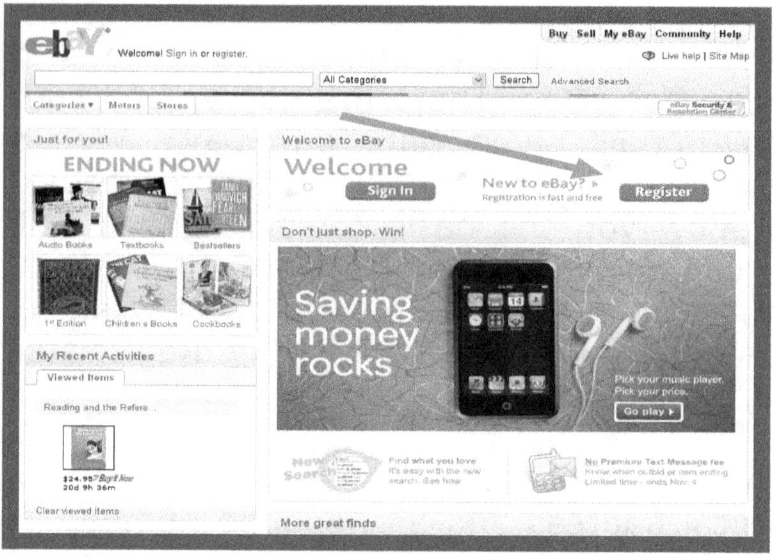

When the registration page appears, enter the following information:

- First name and last name
- Street address (including city, state, ZIP code, and country)
- Telephone numbers primary (required) and secondary (optional)
- Date of birth
- Email address

On the Enter Information page, scroll down and study the eBay User Agreement and Privacy Policy, and check the box to show your affirmation to both agreements, and then click the Continue button.

When the Choose User ID and Password page appears, select one of the user names that eBay suggests for you, or create and enter your own user ID into the Create Your Own ID box.

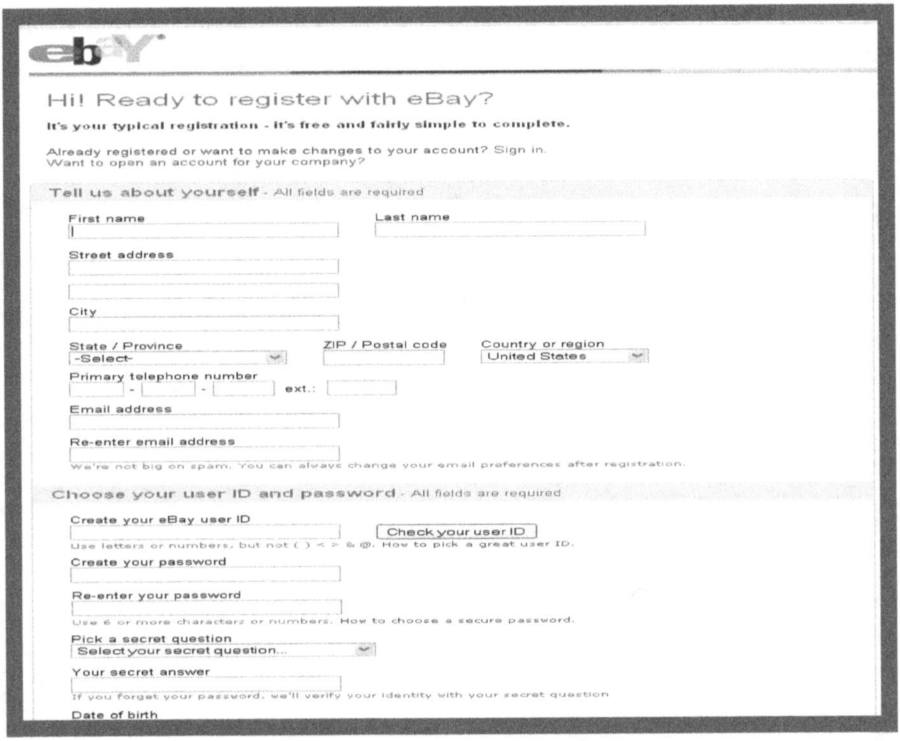

Still on the same page, create and enter a secure password (at least six characters long, with no spaces) into the *Create Password* box. Repeat the password again into the *Re-Enter Password* box. On the same page, select a question from the *Secret Question* list, and then enter your answer in the *Secret Answer* box.

Click on the *Continue button* when done, EBay will now verify your email address and sends you a confirmation message via your email, like the one shown in the following image. When you receive the confirmation email, click the *Activate Your eBay Membership* link in the email message to finalize the registration process. Now, you can start buying or selling on eBay.

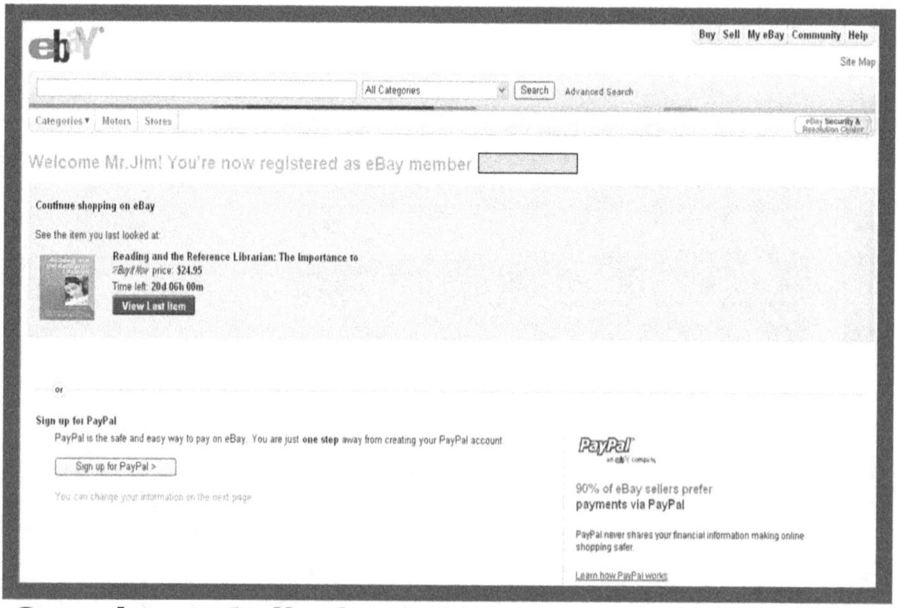

Creating a Seller's Account

If you plan to sell products on eBay, you will need to provide a little bit more information to eBay, in particular, your checking account number and a credit or debit card number.

The credit/debit card number is for billing purposes; your card is billed for all sellers' fees you might incur after selling products. (You can also select to pay via checking account withdrawal; eBay bills your account once in a month.)

The checking account information will confirm that you are the bona fide user, just to weed out fraudulent sellers from the system. During this one-time process, you will need to provide information to verify your identity and select how you will pay your seller fees.

To become a seller on E Bay, you will need to

- Verify your identity and address
- Select the way and manner to pay your seller fees
- Offer Papal or a Merchant Account Credit Card, as a payment method

To help provide a safe and secure environment for the eBay community, you will need to provide a credit or debit card to create a seller's account.

If you do not have a credit card with you or do not want to place your card on file, you can establish your proof of identity with the following link.

There is a charge for verification and it is valid until your name, home address, or phone number change. You may pay the fees only when you complete the process.

http://pages.ebay.com/services/buyandsell/idverify-login.html

Verify your identity by providing your credit card information

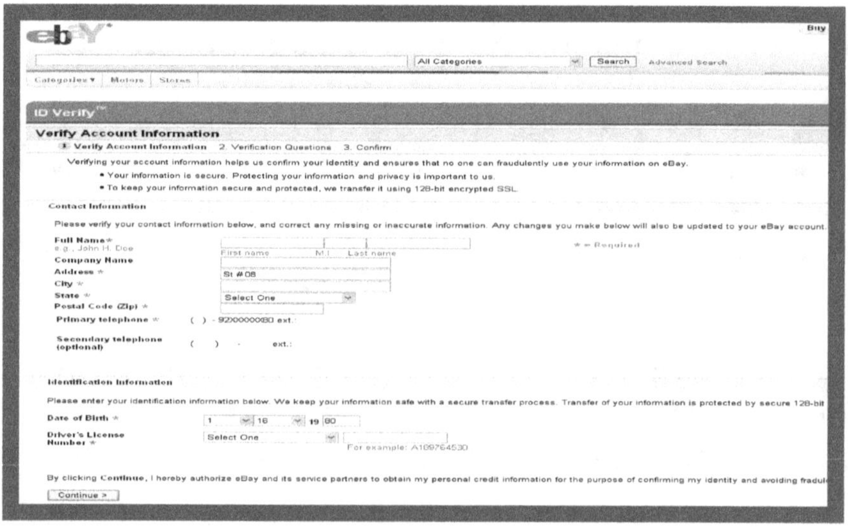

You may need to pay any fees, unless you authorize eBay to use it to pay your seller fees, which are charged, only when you list or sell items.

When becoming a seller, you will need to select how you pay your seller fees. You can pay your seller fees by using any of the following payment methods:

- PayPal (monthly and one-time payments)
- Credit Card (monthly and one-time payments)
- Direct Pay from your checking account (monthly and one-time payments)
- Check (business only)

To select how to pay click here following linhttp://cgi4.ebay.com/ws/eBayISAPI.dll?SellerSignIn

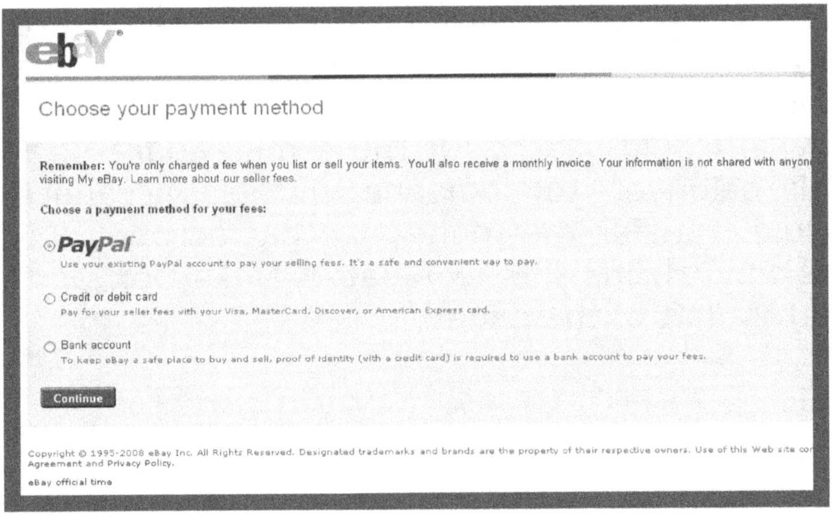

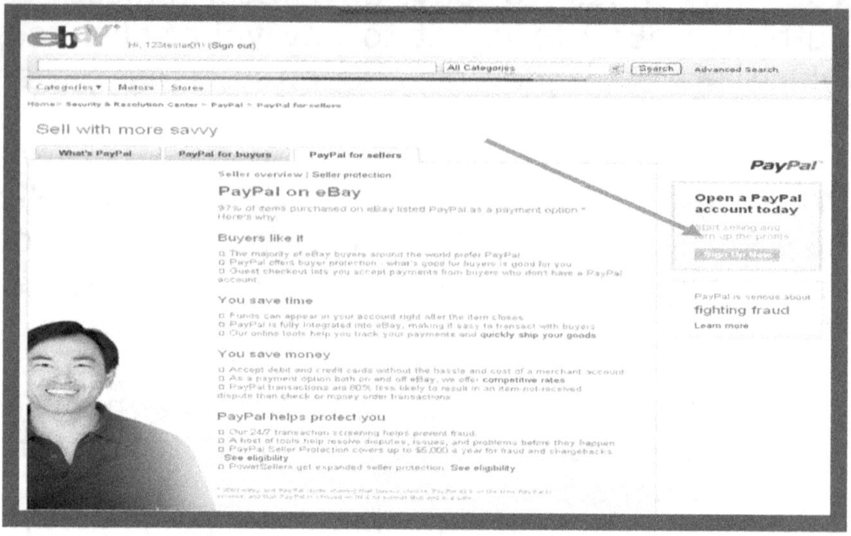

The best way for new eBay merchants to collect money is by using PayPal. PayPal, an Internet startup in 1998, created a simple payment system that allowed individuals to e-mail money to one another. Members could "load" their account on PayPal with money, and then instruct PayPal to a particular e-mail address a certain amount of money.

PayPal would search for the e-mail address, and if it belonged to someone with an account, it would transfer the money to that account. Click the PayPal link in the Related Links box at the bottom left of the page.

Registering for a PayPal account

Click the *Sign Up for a PayPal Account* button.

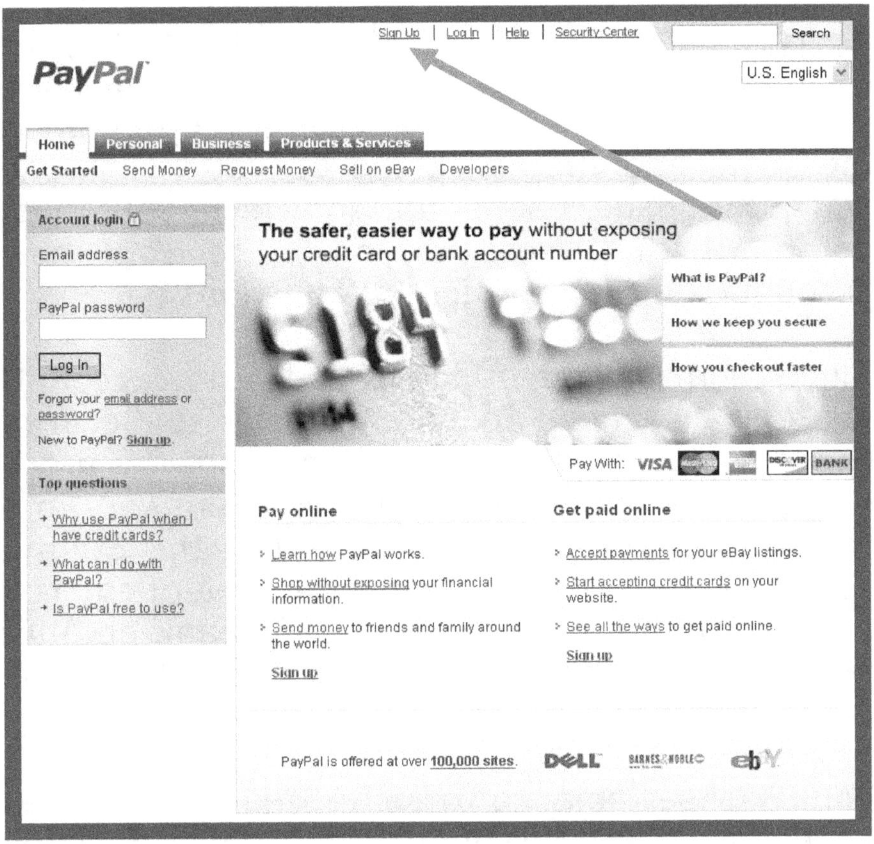

Create an account *Password* you must use at least eight characters and later click the check box at the bottom of the page.

This will ask you to acknowledge that you have read the Privacy Policy and User Agreement. Now, click the *Register* link at the bottom of the page.

A fresh page appears telling you that your account has been set up. You are not finished yet. Check your e-mail for a confirmation message, and then click the activation link. An activation page opens up, in which you must enter your password to log in to your new account. Now, enter Security questions page.

Almost similar to setting up your eBay account, you will also need to enter answer to Security Questions. Choose two questions from the drop-down list box, and then type your answers into the Answer boxes. When you click the Submit button, your account is currently unverified. You can verify the account by adding bank-account information; you may also want to add credit-card information, too.

You will be able to transfer money between PayPal and your accounts. **C**lick the *Add bank account Bank Name, Account Type, Routing Number, and Account Number*. Then click the *Add Bank Account* button at the bottom of the page.

Though the process is still incomplete, it actually is not. You will still need to wait for some days because PayPal will place, a couple of small deposits into your bank account (only a few cents).
When you see the deposit—in a statement, online, or through phone banking, perhaps—log back into your PayPal account and click the *Confirm Bank Account* link that appears, and then enter the amounts deposited (thus proving you have access to the account).

To set up link a credit card to your account, follow a similar procedure, beginning with clicking the *Add credit card* link. This process only takes a few moments with eBay contacting the credit-card network to verify the card. PayPal provides a number of services to assist and protect eBay merchants, including the following:

- Automatic PayPal logo insertion
- Offer PayPal Buyer Credit
- Seller Protection Policy
- Invoicing
- Shipping Center
- ATM/Debit Card

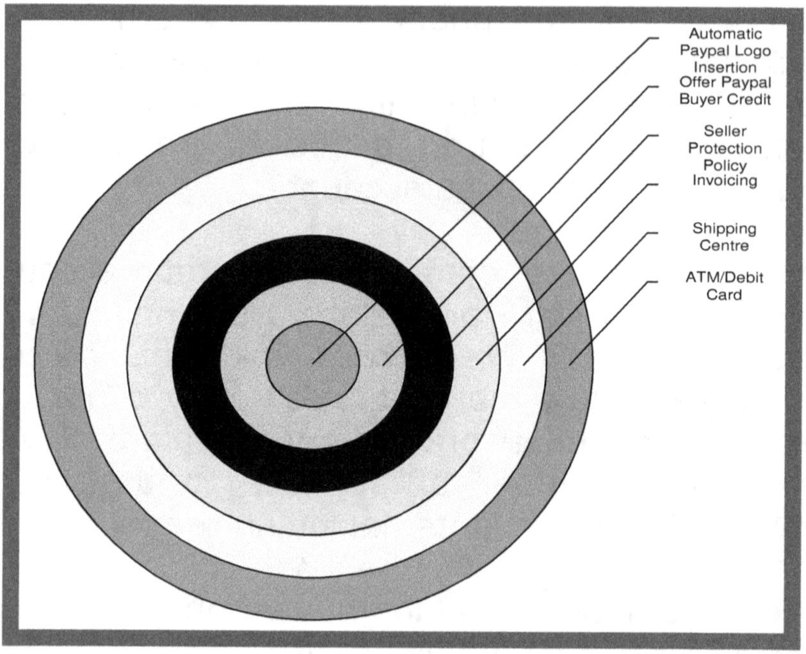
Automatic Paypal Logo Insertion
Offer Paypal Buyer Credit
Seller Protection Policy
Invoicing
Shipping Centre
ATM/Debit Card

Overview for eBay Home Page

The eBay home page is the starting or launching point for all your eBay action.
From this one simple screen, you can get to all the places you will ever want to go on eBay.

- Navigation
- Search
- Specialty Sites
- Categories

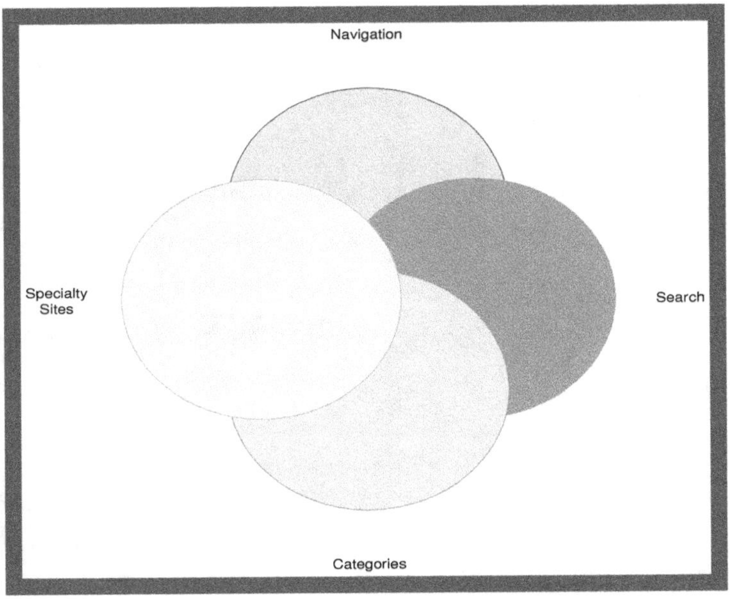

Search

You can use the *"what are you looking for Box"* to find the products and services that you always wanted to buy. Type words that describe the goods you are looking for and then click *Find It*. To do an advanced search (that is, to search by price range, category, and similar features), click the *Smart Search* link.

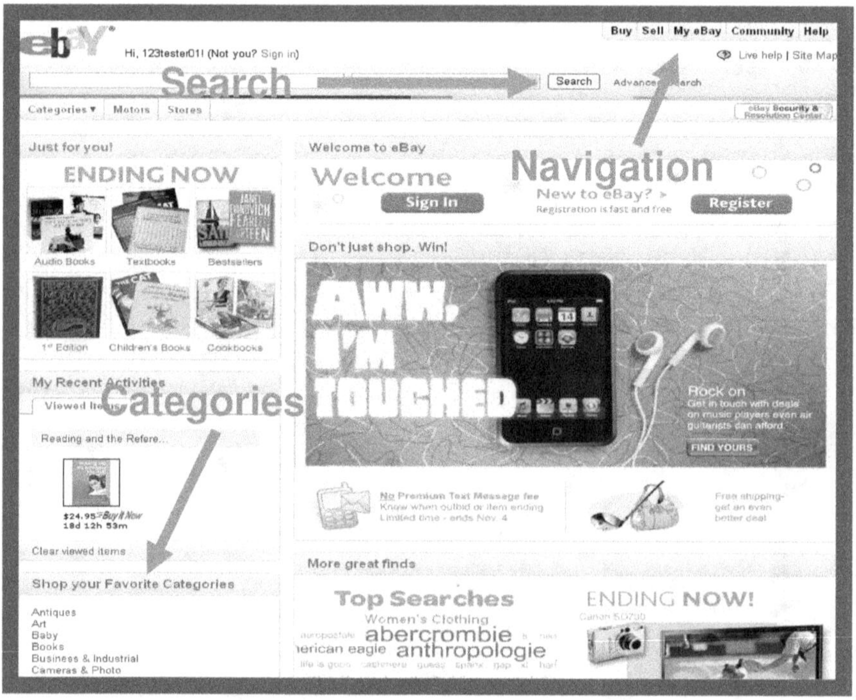

Specialty Sites

EBay is a great find-it-all and buy-whatever-you-want type of auction site. It is now comprised of a number of related sites as well, and this portion of the page lets you navigate to them. EBay Motors provides you an opportunity to buy and sell cars, motorcycles, boats, and car parts.

Stores

They provide a number of links to a number of traditional online stores, where you can buy directly from the store at a fixed price.
This will help you avoid competing against other buyers at an auction.

Half.com is a bargain-hunting site with great deals on everything including computers, books, games, and electronics. No bidding is here as well, just see what you like and buy! In addition, PayPal is the best way for paying your sellers, when you win an auction, or for being paid from buyers, if you are selling at an auction.

Categories

Travel here to browse through all of eBay's auction categories—from antiques to travel and everything in the world.

Navigation

The navigation bar is at the top of the eBay home page and it lists five eBay links that take you directly to any of the different eBay areas. Using the navigation bar is just like one-stop clicking. You can find this bar at the top of every page that you visit on eBay. When you click one of the five links, you get another sub-navigation bar with specific links to other related important places.

Here are the five navigation bar links:

Sell

The link takes you to the *"sell your item form"*, that you fill out to start listing your items for auctions.

My eBay

This links takes you to your personal My eBay page, where you can keep track of all your buying and selling activities, account information, and favorite categories.

Community

By taking this link, you can travel to a page, where you can find the latest news and announcements, chat with fellow traders in the eBay community, find charity auctions, and find out more about eBay.

How Can I Create About Me Page?

You can remain relatively anonymous and invisible on the eBay system, or you can choose to tell everyone a little bit about yourself, via an *About Me* page. An *About Me* page will have personal information, auction listings, feedback listings, and links to your favorite pages on the Web.

When you are ordering for a product or listing your product for auctions, you have not yet established your reputation, as displayed by your feedback rating pages. Now, you can use your *About Me* page to tell potential buyers and sellers a little more about yourself, who can help offset any dubious opinions, they may have of your low feedback rating.

Make sure that your *About Me* page is as professional as possible, so that you can leave a good impression.
You do not have to be a professional web programmer to create your own *About Me* page. You can easily create your own *About Me* page by following the following simple steps. On any eBay page, click the Site Map link (above the Navigation Bar).

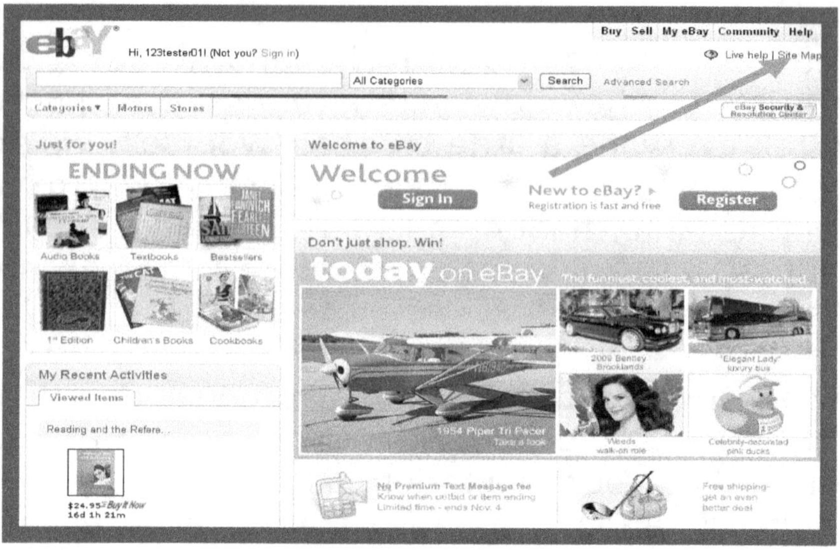

When the Site Map page appears in front of you, go to the *Connect* section and click *About Me*

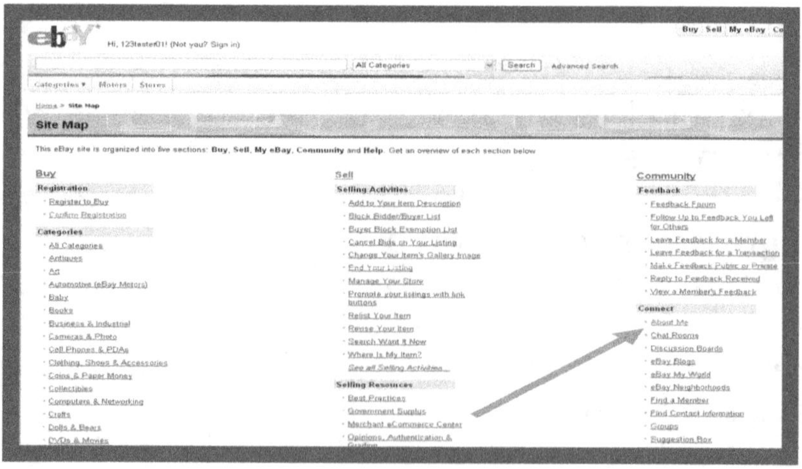

When you see the *About Me* page, click on Click Here button.

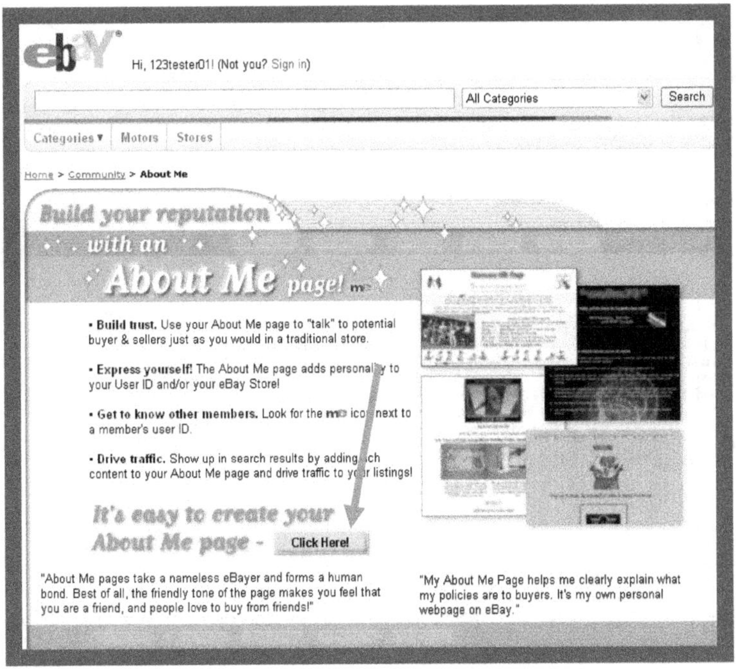

When the next page appears, click on the *Create Your Page* button.

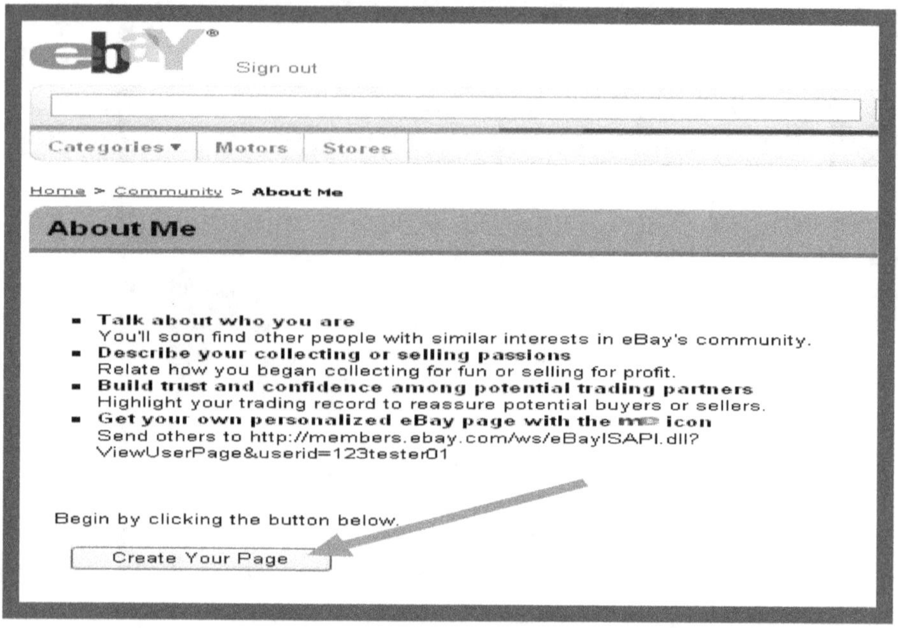

When the: *"Choose Your Editing Option"* page comes up, check the *Use Our Easy Step-by-Step Process* option, then click the *Continue* button.

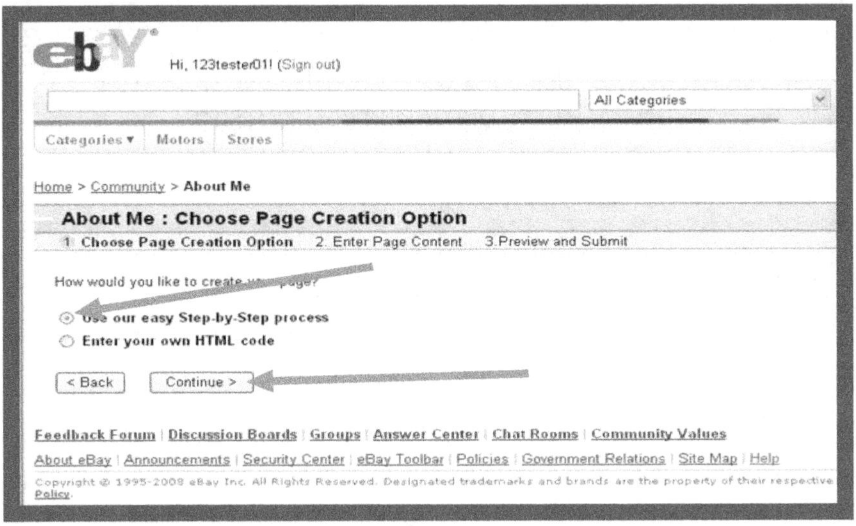

When the *"Enter Page Content"* page comes up, as shown in the following figure, start by entering a precise title into the *Page Title* box. On the same page, you can now enter two paragraphs of information, using the supplied formatting controls or (by clicking the Enter Your Own HTML link) with your HTML codes.

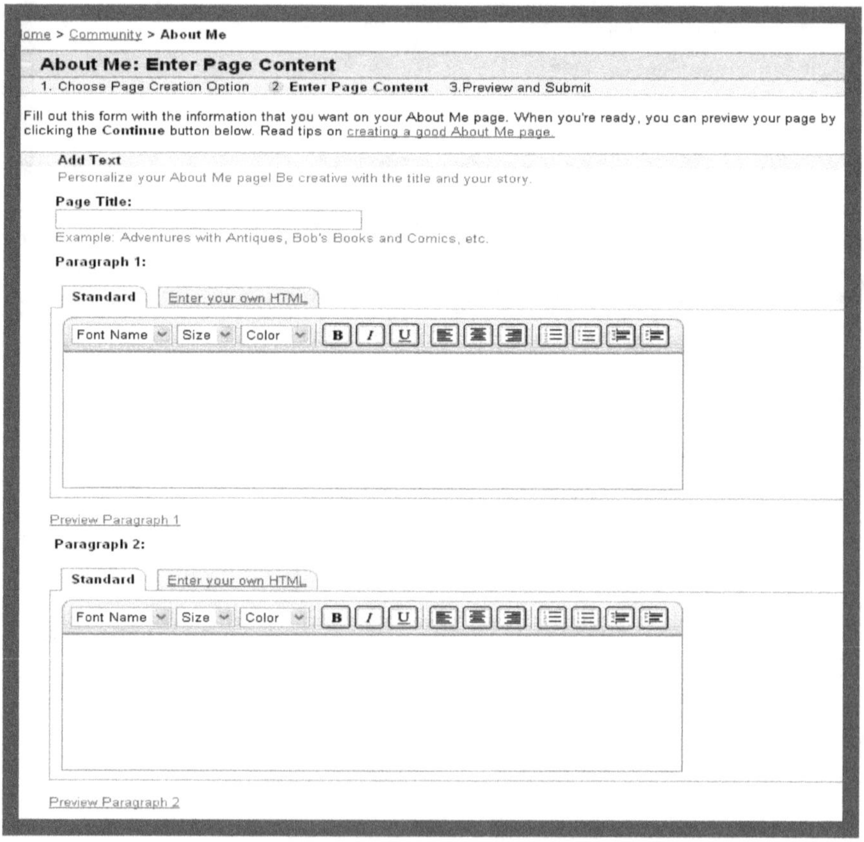

On the same page, enter a URL to establish a link to any picture you want to include on your page, as well as an optional description title for the picture.

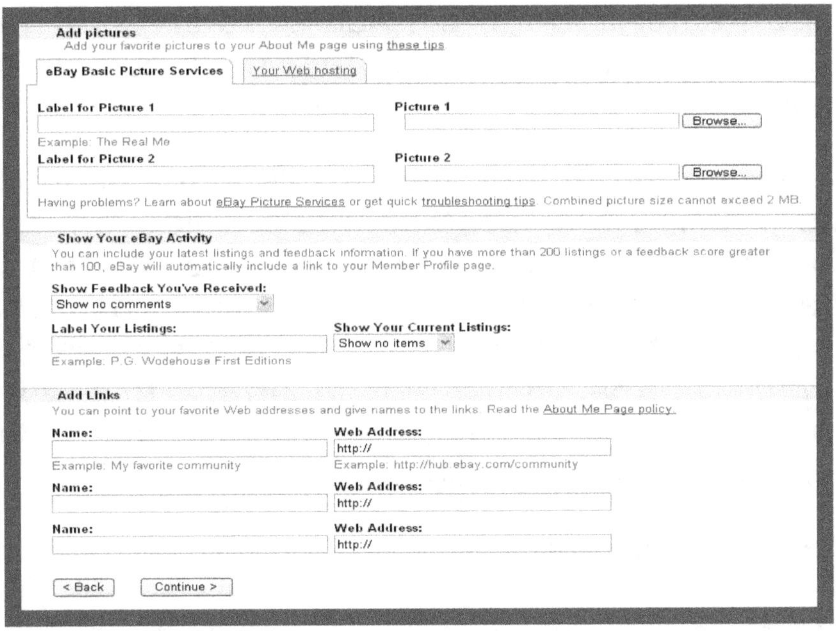

In the *Show your eBay activity* section, choose the number of feedback comments and current auction listings you want to display on the page.

If you want to include any links to external web pages, enter them in the Add Links section. This will help you advertise you to a large number of people.

When you finish entering all this information on the *Enter Page Content* page, click on the *Continue* button to go the next page. When the *Preview and Submit* page appears, choose a good layout for your page, and then click on the *Submit* button. It is too important that your *About Me* page actually be about you, your personal likes and dislikes.

Online Auctions

The perceived value of an item or product is determined by the amount of money someone is willing to spend to buy it. That is what makes auctions exciting and thrilling. EBay offers you several kinds of auctions, but for the most part, they all work in the same way. An auction is a unique sales event, where the exact price of the item for sale is unknown to sellers.

As a result, there is an element of surprise and suspense involved not only for the bidder (who might end up with a great and value breaking deal) but also for the seller (who might end up making a large profit). Before you go bidding, buying, and selling, you should get some training in how online auctions actually work. Here are the basics of what you need to know.

Online Auctions for Buyer

When you want to buy something on eBay, the first thing you will usually do is browse through the listings. Listings are by category, such as Coins, Computer & Electronics, or Collectibles. Each category is divided into subcategories, so finding the right type of item you are interested in is very easy.

You can also enter a specific word or phrase to describe the kind of item you are interested in buying, such as a pair of socks. No matter which way you find an item you want to buy, you will navigate to an auction page that describes what is up for sale. You may find both the description and product's image on the page. On a number of auctions, there is also a suggested minimum bidding price. In addition, you will also see the current highest bid as well. If you are interested in bidding on the item, you can enter your bid by filling out a simple online bidding form.

Each auction runs for a specific amount of time. Over that bidding period, people keep on visiting the bid page to bid for the item, so you'll have to keep checking back to check whether anyone has bid higher than you—and later to enter an even higher bid price, if you still want the item at the higher price.

At the end of the auction, the highest bidder and the seller are notified by email and it is up to them to make payment and shipping arrangements. Many sellers ask for some kind of guaranteed form of payment, such as a money order or certified check. There is a lot more to the bidding process, but these points' just covers the basics of E Bay bidding process. For more information about bidding, turn to Part II, "Buying on eBay."

Online Auctions for Seller

When you want to sell something on eBay, it is quite simple and straightforward. Determine your minimum selling price (or decide that there's no minimum price and that you'll accept *any* bid amount), decide in which category your item should go for bidding, and then fill out a form detailing what you have for sale on auction. To make the item more interesting and cajoling, you can add a number of pictures, fancy fonts, and other useful extras to your auction page.

You will have to pay eBay for your listing; the fee to be paid is based on the selling price of the item. At the end of the auction, you will ask the buyer for payment, and you then ship the goods after receiving the products. For more information please read 'Selling on eBay' next pages.

Different Types of Auctions

There are many types of auctions on eBay. Most important are:

- Multiple Item auctions
- Live Auctions
- Reserve-price auctions
- Private auctions

Dutch Auctions / Multiple Item Auctions

Multiple Item auctions (also called Dutch auctions) have nothing to do with windmills. A Multiple Item auction allows a seller to put multiple, identical items up for sale. Instead of holding 100 separate auctions for 100 pairs of wooden shoes, for example, a seller can sell them all in one listing. As a buyer, you can elect to bid for 1, 3, or all 100 pairs.

Live Auctions

If you want that traditional, going-going, gone and disappeared (highest bidder wins) type of auction, you can participate in auctions that are running live, 24x7, at a gallery in real time. In eBay Live Auctions, you can bid via eBay's continuous auction, just as if you were sitting in a chair at the auction house.

These auctions are suggested usually for unique and interesting items that you are not likely to find anywhere else. Following figure shows the Live Auctions home page located at this link www.ebay.com/liveauctions.

Reserve-price auctions

Unlike a minimum bid, which is required in any eBay auction, a reserve price protects sellers from having to sell or dispose an item for less than the minimum amount they want for it. The reserve price allows you to set lower minimum bids, and lower minimum bids always attract bidders. Unfortunately, when a seller makes the reserve price too high, and it is not met by the end of the auction, no one really wins. EBay charges a special fee for sellers to run these auctions. Nobody knows (except the seller and the eBay computer system) what the reserve price is, until the auction is over.

Private Auctions

Some sellers choose to hold private auctions for their products, because they know that some bidders might be embarrassed to be seen bidding on a box of racy neckties, in front of the rest of the eBay bidders. Others might choose the private route, because they are selling big-ticket items and do not want to disclose their bidders' financial status. Private auctions are just like the typical timed auctions, except that each bidder's identity is secret. At the end of the auction, eBay provides buyer's contact info to the seller and to the high bidder.

How can we perform a search?

If you have something more specific in mind to sell, say a pair of neckties, which cost between $10 and $25, you may have to carry out a search. Doing a search for a particular product can be as simple as typing a simple search term or as complex as performing a complex search, in which you specify a price range, an auction location, and other criteria, such as only ties. Here, you will learn how to do a search and then to sort and segregate the completed search in detail, so you can cull out the products as quickly as possible.

Depending on how many auctions eBay finds that match your search term, it might return a page with many categories and subcategories of relevant auctions, rather than listing individual auctions. You will also see how many categories and subcategories match your search. There can be hundreds of categories and subcategories and many thousands of matching items.

Many a time, a good way to refine and localize a search is to sort it by categories. On the left side of the results page, you will find a *Matching Categories* section (drop down list), with a list of the categories, where matching items were found.

Next to each category is a number, which is the total number of auctions in that category that match your search. Click the category to display only the items in that category that match your search.

When you narrow down your search, you will see a listing of all the auctions that match your search terms. Scroll through the auctions, until you find one you are interested in; then click it to get details and bid.

How can I sort my search?

Searching for an item is just the first step toward finding a product on which you might want to bi; eBay has so many numbers of auctions going on simultaneously, that you will commonly find hundreds of matching and similar auctions, even after narrowing the search. That is where sorting your searches useful. By smartly sorting your searches, you will be able to focus easily on items you want to bid on, for example, by narrowing your search to only specific categories, or to only auctions that are about to end.

Option-1

When you first see your search results, you will observe auctions as well as, *Buy It Now* items. To see just auctions, click the *Auctions* tab at the top of the results page, and to see *Buy It Now* items only, click the *Buy It Now* tab.

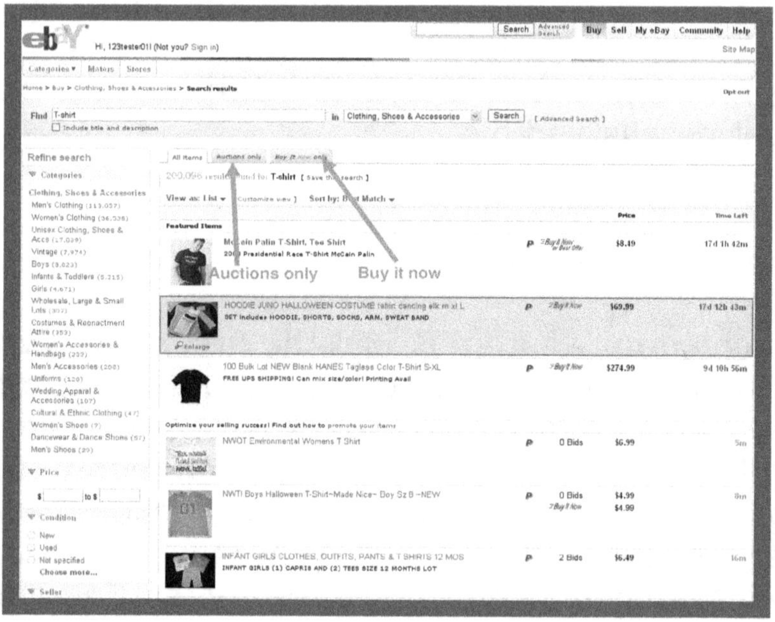

Option-2

You can easily sort the search results, so they are listed with the highest priced items first or the lowest-priced items first, by clicking either the *lowest priced* ***or*** *highest priced* link. To see those auctions that are closest to ending, click the *ending first link*, and to see those auctions listed recently, click the *newly listed* link.

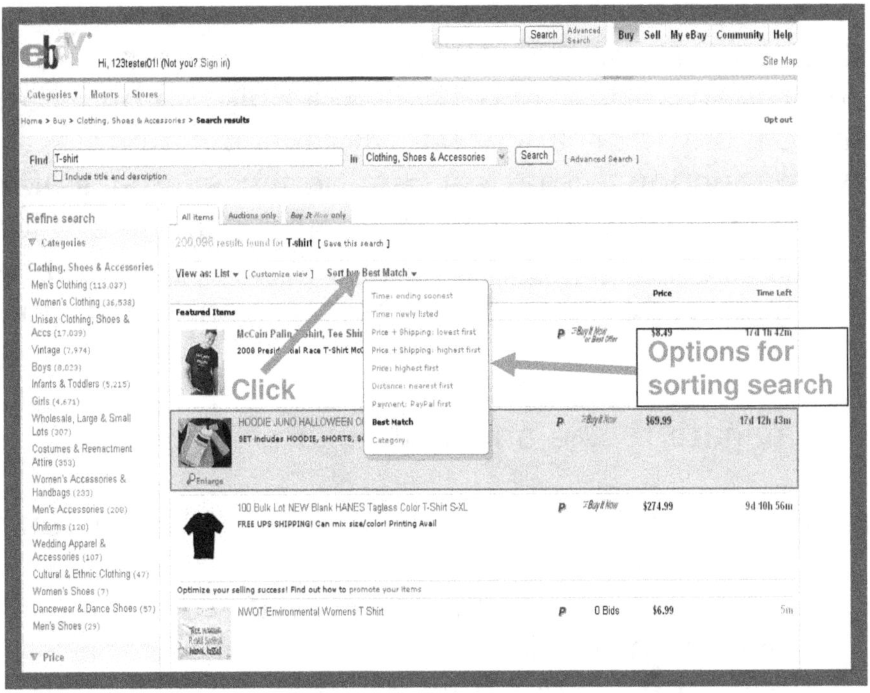

Advanced Search

Sometimes, simple searches are not just enough there are so much information on eBay and so many countless items for sale that even doing intelligent searches with good sorting does not provide the best result. That is when you need to perform an advanced search.

With an advanced search, you can perform very fine-tuned searches—for example, you can search only for auctions, by specific people or even auctions that accept only a particular currency. If you are searching for specialty items, you will find that advanced searches are the best way to find what you want, fast and immediately.

To navigate to the advanced search page:

- Click the search button on the top of any eBay page.
- Click the advanced search tab.
- Fill in basic search information
- Use the simple search box and basic search screen to type your search term, category, price range, and similar information.

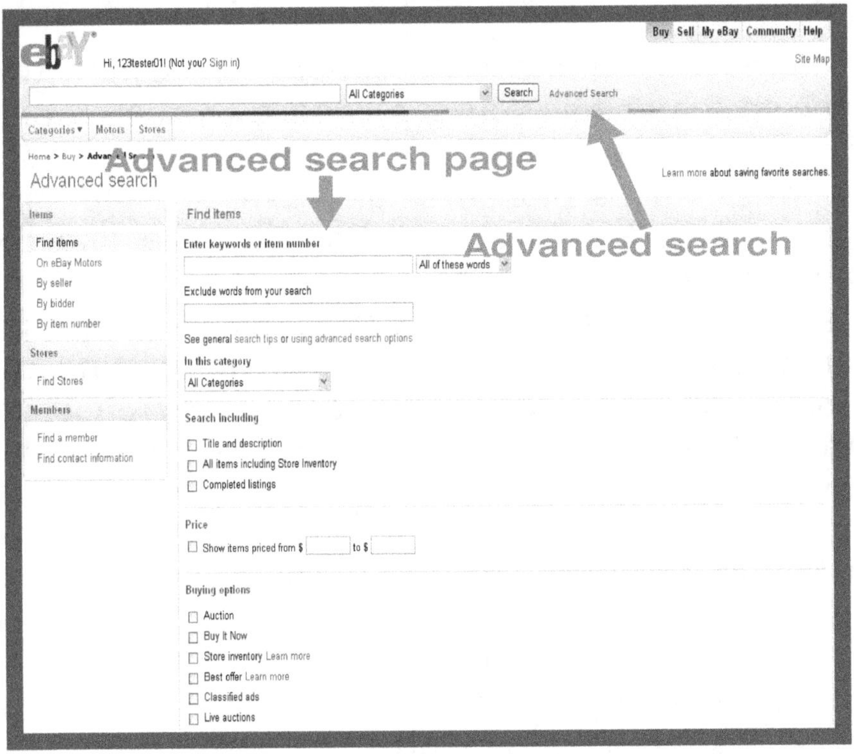
Buy Sell My eBay Community Help
Hi, 123tester01! (Not you? Sign in)
Site Map
All Categories
Search
Advanced Search
Categories Motors Stores
Advanced search page
Advanced search
Learn more about saving favorite searches.
Items
Find items
On eBay Motors
By seller
By bidder
By item number
Stores
Find Stores
Members
Find a member
Find contact information
Find items
Enter keywords or item number
All of these words
Advanced search
Exclude words from your search
See general search tips or using advanced search options
In this category
All Categories
Search including
Title and description
All items including Store Inventory
Completed listings
Price
Show items priced from $ to $
Buying options
Auction
Buy It Now
Store inventory Learn more
Best offer Learn more
Classified ads
Live auctions

Advanced Search Options

You have a number of options for conducting power searching. You can choose to search only through gift auctions, Buy It Now items, auctions in which more than a single item is up for bid, and so on. Select your options by enabling the applicable check boxes next to *Item type*. You can also choose the number of results to display on each page (25, 50, or 100), determine the sort order, and set similar options by choosing from the drop-down lists under the display format heading.

Here are following search options.

- Search by seller
- Search by buyer
- Search by eBay stores

Search by Seller/Buyer

Click the *'By Seller'* tab to search for items being auctioned by a particular seller. You would also want to do this, if you have dealt with a particular seller in the past and feel she offers good auctions. First, fill in the seller ID. After you fill in the seller's ID, you can customize the search in a number of ways, such as changing or altering the way the results are sorted.

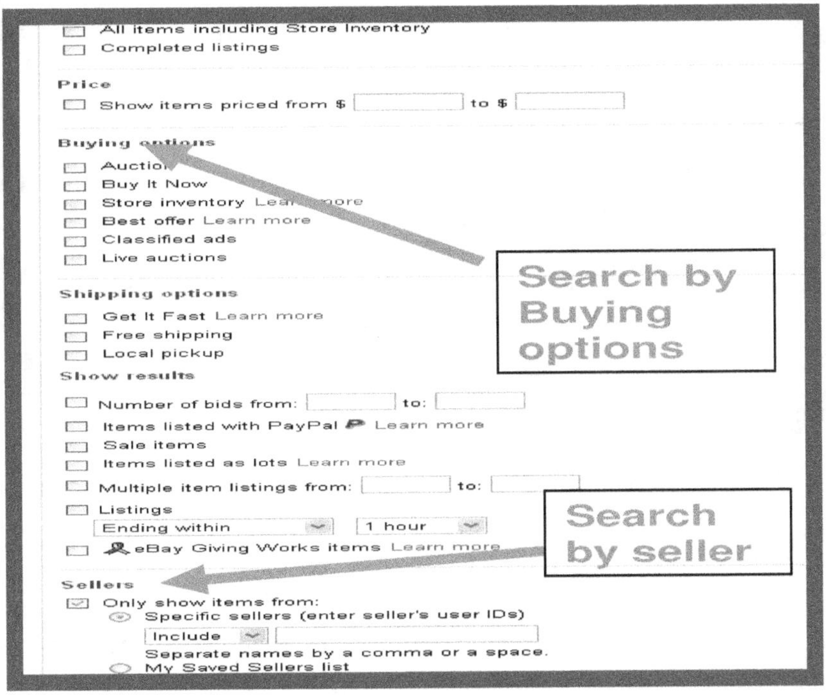

Search by eBay Stores

Click the *Stores* tab to search for items, products and services in eBay stores. EBay stores are online, accomplished storefronts run by high-volume and power eBay sellers. They frequently offer *Buy It Now* items and accept credit card payments.

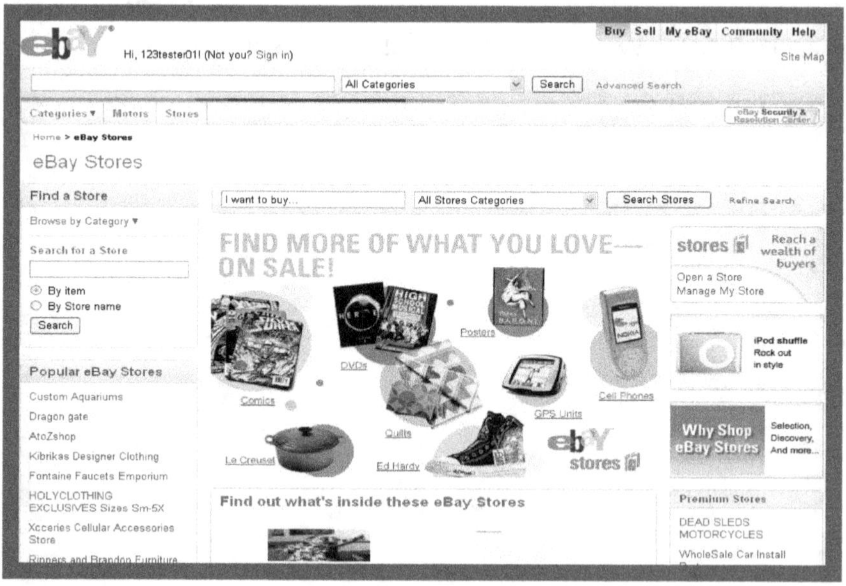

Search for eBay Members

When you buy something on eBay, you are often buying or selling in a blind manner.
However, eBay offers ways you can find information about a seller and ways you can find contact information for the seller, so you can get directly in touch with the buyer.

Here is how to do it.

Go to the *Find Members* Page from any eBay page; click the search button at the top of a page and then click the find member's button.

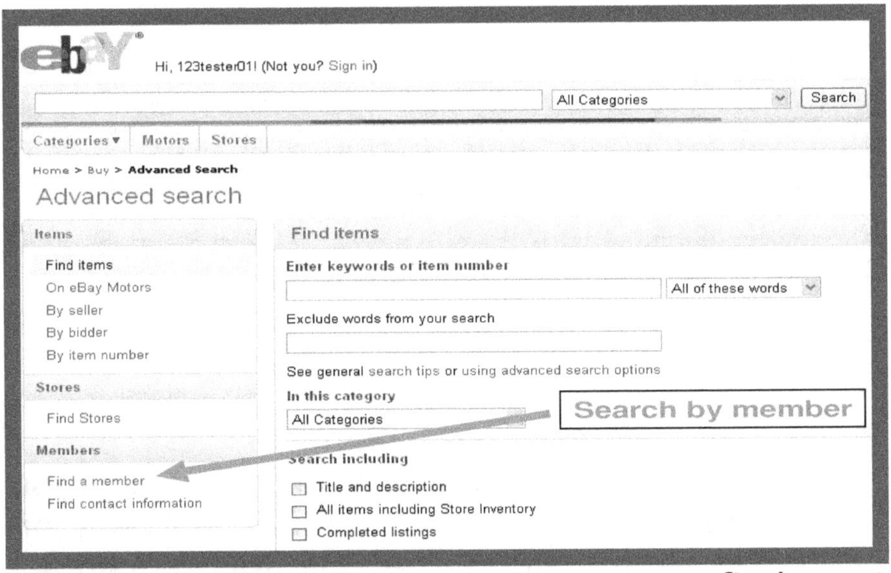

Please note: *Before you can find out information about a particular member, you must find his member ID. If you have forgotten it for some reason, scroll to the bottom of the page and type the email address of the member; then enter the four-digit number displayed on the page and click Search.* If you do not know the exact email address or the ID of the member, you will not be able to get information about him.

If eBay finds a member with the email address you have specified, you will navigate to the member's *Feedback Profile* page. At the top of the page will be the member's ID.

Member's Feedback Profile Page

To see the full profile and past record of feedback about a member, type the member ID in the *Feedback Profile* section and press enter. The *Feedback Profile* page is possibly the best place to see how other eBay buyers rate this person's transactions with previous buyers.

Contact Information

If you are a seller and want to get contact information about a number of bidders, or if you are a bidder and want to get contact information about the seller, you can request for the contact information from eBay.
Go to the contact info section of the find member's page and type the member ID and the item number of the auction you are either bidding on or using to sell an item. Click the submit button when you are finished.

Save Your Search

Many buyers who use eBay everyday look for almost the same types of items to buy—for example, books, garments or cloth or shoes. Therefore, eBay offers you a convenient and easiest way to easily find those item; you can create a search and then save that search, so that rather than typing in a new search every time, you can just go back to a particular search that you've already saved. Soon after this, eBay will do the search again and returns fresh and new items. **Y**ou may also wish to save a search, if you are looking for a particular item, then could not find it, but want to check again. Simply save your search, revisit it, and eBay will do the search again, checking to see whether any new items are there for sale, after the last time you have searched. You can perform a simple search or an advanced search; it does not really matter. You can save any kind of search. After you see the results for the search and are satisfied with the product the search options have returned, you can now save the search.

At the top of the search results page, click the *Add to My Favorite Searches* link. A page appears now, asking you to give the search a specific name. Type a search name that is as descriptive and self-explanatory as possible and then click the *Submit* button.

You can save up to 100 separate searches in this manner. You can save not just searches alone, but page browses as well. **F**or example, you might want to get to a particular subcategory, such as hand woven silk ties. To add a favorite category, in the *My Favorite Categories* area of the *Favorite Searches* page, click *Add/Change categories*, select the categories you want to follow, and click *Submit*.

Searching sites online

If you do not find the information that you need at eBay, do not lose your patience. Even a site as vast and voluminous as eBay does not have a full monopoly on products information. The Internet is full of Web sites and Internet auction sites that can provide you price comparisons and information about a number of cyber-clubs. Your home computer can connect to powerful external servers (big computers on the Internet) that have their own fast-searching systems called *search engines.* Remember, if something is out there and you need it, you can find it right from your home computer in just a matter of seconds.

Here are some of the addresses of the Web's most highly regarded and famous search engines or multi-search-engine sites.

- AltaVista (www.altavista.com)

- Dogpile (www.dogpile.com)
- Excite (www.excite.com)
- Google (www.google.com)
- Yahoo! (www.yahoo.com)
- Ask (www.ask.com)

The basic mechanism of culling information from an Internet search engine is quite simple:

Type the address of the search-engine site in the Address box of your Web browser. Find the text box next to the button labeled Search or something similar.

In the text box, type a few words indicating what interests you. Be quite specific when entering the search text. The more precise your entry is, the better your chances are of finding what you really want. Look for tips, an advanced search option, or help pages on your search engine of choice for more information about how to narrow your search. Click the Search (or similar) button or press Enter on your keyboard. The search engine presents you with a list of the Internet pages that have the requested information.

The list includes a number of brief descriptions and links to the first set of pages. You will find links to additional listings at the bottom of the page, if your search arrives at more listings than can fit on one page.

Always treat the information on the web with utmost caution. Not everyone is the type of expert that he or she would like or want to be. If you are looking for prices to buy a car or a bike on eBay, study your local newspaper to get a fair idea of prevailing prices in your community.

PART 2

Buying on eBay

Buying products and services on eBay consists of two simple and straightforward steps:

- Finding a product or service you want to buy
- Bidding and winning the item

Nevertheless, how to we find what exactly we want to buy? Usually, the easiest way is to browse or search for it by going through a series of different categories, until you get to a comprehensive list of your interest. However, keep in mind: Never get distracted by those highlighted and accented auctions that you will come to when you first arrive at eBay. Nevertheless, remember for what purpose you came to the site, and then start your browsing by category.

Finding an Item

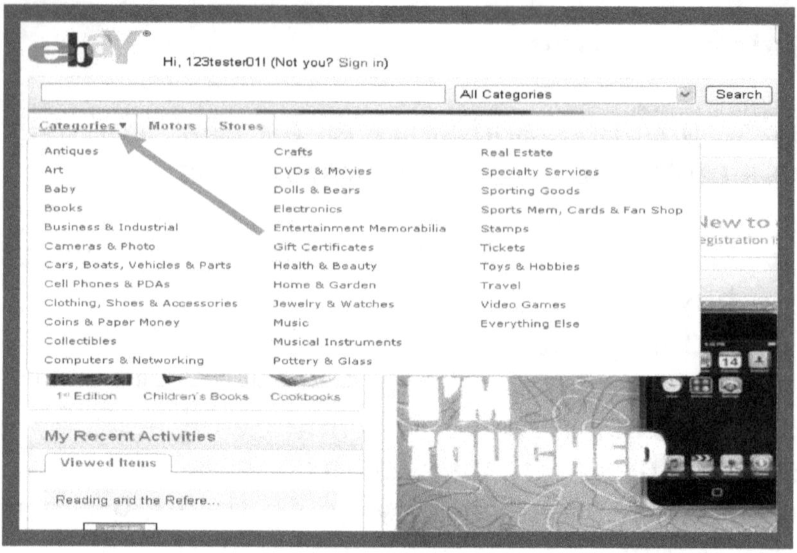

Step-1

On the left side of eBay's main page, look for the list of Categories. The main categories are in larger type and boldfaced, whereas the subcategories of those categories are in smaller, non-boldface type. Very few subcategories are listed, so unless you see and search for a subcategory, you may find it very difficult to find the products of your choice.

Step-2

Depending on the chosen category, the category page might look different from, what is displayed here. For some category pages, the entire screen is dominated by the subcategories; in others, the subcategories are simply listed down the left side. After you select the subcategory, you can see a list of all the pending auctions in that subcategory, although in some cases, you might see more number of subcategories.

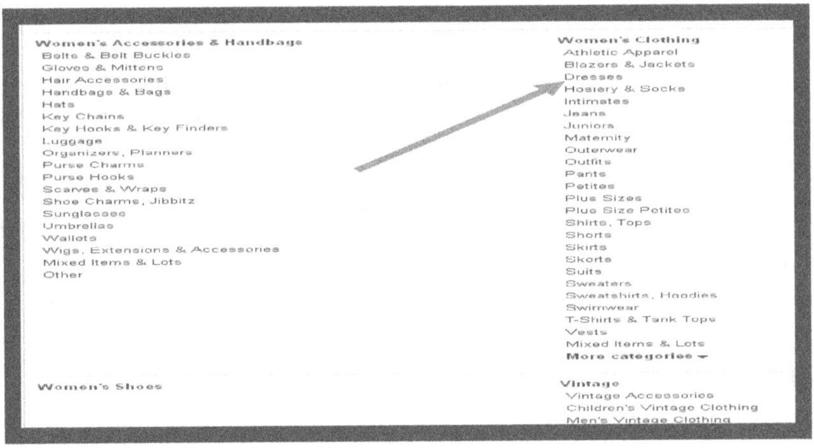

Select the Auction

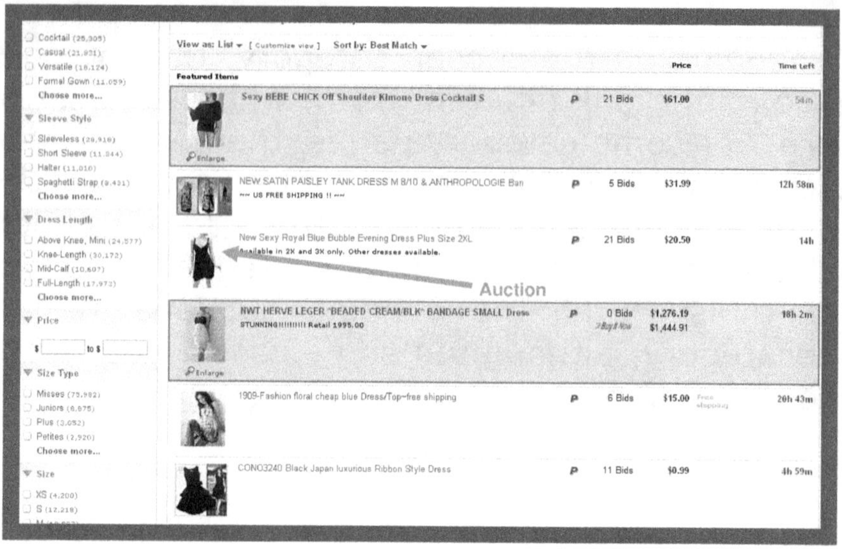

Now scroll through the entire auction listings until you find one you want to bid. If you want to see auctions that are about to end, click the going, going, and gone (soon to disappear type of auctions) link at the top of the listings. To check the auctions that end today, click on *ending today link*. To see the auctions begun today, click on *new today* link.

Read the Auction Page

The auction page provides you details about the pending auction, information about the seller, gives a link that allows you to ask seller a question, and later helps you bid on the item.

Browse by Region, Theme, and Store

You can also browse in many other ways, instead of by category alone. Click on the Browse button at the top of the eBay page to see a list of other browsing options. In addition to browsing by categories, you can click a number of buttons to browse by regions, themes, and stores.

Browsing by region allows you watch and see items being sold in specific geographic areas. Browsing by themes lets you browse by themes, such as cloth, electronics or motors. Browsing by stores lets you browse by various online retail outlets.

Quick Search for Auction

If you want to buy an item quickly, there is an easier and faster way to find it than just by browsing through the categories. You should use eBay's quick search feature instead. The search box is there on literally every eBay page. To use it, enter the phrase, word or words that describe the item you are searching.

Make your search as focused and specific as possible. However, be sure not to make the search too narrow and focused; otherwise, you may overlook some items of importance.

Here are some other important tips that you can follow to ensure that you spend the least time searching for items of your choice:

- Delete or add the letter s to your search.
- Use quotation marks to search for exact phrases.
- You do not have to use the word 'and' on eBay.
- Use a comma and no space, if you want to use the word or.
- Use the – sign to narrow your searching.
- Sort the items by ending date, bid price, or search ranking.

An overview on Auctions Page

The auction page is your command page for buying on e Bay, it contains everything that you need to know about items on sale, who is selling them, how much it's being sold for, and the terms of the sale. Here are the most important parts of the auction page:

- Basic Auction Information
- Buy it Now Price
- Seller Information
- History
- Time Left
- Shipping
- Payment Methods

- High Bidder
- Quantity
- Location

Basic auction information

In this section, you can see the current high bid, the amount of time left until the auction ends, how many bids have been received for that item, which the high bidder is, and the location of the seller. With this section, you can get more details about the bidding history just by clicking the link next to 'history'. Now, you can see a list of every bid made for the item, the date of bidding, and who actually made it. You can also send an email to the current high bidder by clicking the bidder's name.

Buy It Now Price

If you want the item now and the price quoted in this area is passable to you, you can immediately click the *Buy It Now* link, which takes you to a sales page, where you can complete your purchase.

Seller Information

Just as important as what you are buying is, whom you are buying from, this section lets you check out the details about the seller.

Here, you can read a summary about the seller's feedback, find out when she or he registered on eBay, see what other items are up for sale, read all the feedback about the seller, and send the buyer an email to ask a specific question. Click the links in the seller area to find details about this information.

History

This link tells you how many bids are there on an item. To use the number of bids to your maximum advantage, you have to know and understand the secrets. You can determine just how hot an item is, just by comparing the number of bids that the item has received over time. Based on the amount of interest shown for an item, you can devise a time strategy.

The starting bid is always listed in light gray next to the total number of bids. If you click on the number of bids, you can find out who is bidding and what date and time bids were placed on this item. The dollar amount of each bid is kept secret until the end of the auction.

Time Left

Although the clock never stops ticking at eBay, you must continue to refresh your browser to see the time remaining on the official clock.

When the item gets down to the last hour of the auction, you see the time in minutes and seconds.

Shipping

Here is where you will find out the shipping costs for a product and who pays for it (most of the time, it is the buyer). For some products, you might also be required to pay shipping insurance (see About Shipping and Insurance).

Payment methods

This page provides you the various ways you can pay for your products: with a personal check, with PayPal, with a money order, with a cashier's check, and other methods. (For more details, please see payment methods next pages.)

High Bidder

This link shows you the User ID and feedback rating of the current highest bidder. Bidding is more of an art than a science. Sometimes, an item gets no bids because everyone is waiting until the last minute of bid. You may see a flurry of activity, as bidders all try to outbid each other (called *sniping*). Nevertheless, that is all part of the fun of eBay. Enter the amount of money you are willing to pay and click the *Place Bid* button.

Quantity

This link appears only in a multiple item fixed-price sale or Multiple Item auction (also called a Dutch auction). It will tell you how many items are available right now.

Location

This link informs you the country where the seller is located, and you might see specific info, like the city and geographic area where the seller is now. Consider the geographic location of a seller when you are bidding on an item. Knowing exactly where the item is can help you quickly calculate the shipping charges and the delivery time.

Please Note Before Placing a Bid

You think about placing a bid on an item to calculate financial obligation that you have to make. In every case, the maximum bid that you place will not be all that you spend on an item. I recommend that you look closely at the payment methods that the seller is willing to accept as well as the shipping costs, insurance costs, and escrow costs. (Before placing a bid, please see Payment Methods, Shipping/Insurance Cost, Feedback next pages.)

In particular, make sure that you get proper and satisfactory answers to questions like these:

- Is the item new or used?
- Is the item a first edition or a reprint? Is it an original or a reissue?
- Is the item in its original packaging? Does it still have the original tags attached?
- Is the item under warranty?

- Before contacting the seller, find out whether other eBay customers who have done business with the buyer trust him or her. In the *Seller Information* area on the auction page, click the *Feedback reviews* link. You will navigate to a page with a summary of feedback ratings about the seller.

  First, go to the top of the page and read a summary of all the reviews—organized by positive, neutral, and negative—over the last seven days, last month, and last six months. If you see too many negative reviews, refrain from bidding on the auction.

- Scroll down the feedback page until you see the actual written feedback from each user. You will also see the names of the people giving the feedback to the buyer;

if you wish, you can click on the linked number next to their names to see the feedback about them, to help you judge whether you should have trust on their feedback.

☞ Back in the *Seller Information* section on the auction page, click on the *Ask seller a question* link. Fill out the form that appears and click the *Send message* button at the bottom of the form to send email to the seller. The auction number is put into the Subject line of the email automatically, so you do not have to do that yourself.

☞ Now you will need to be very patient! How long does the seller take to respond to your question? Did he or she answer the question fully and in a satisfactory manner? Did you get enough extra information and details, which enables you to bid on the item? If the seller is not responsive and enthusiastic before the sale of item, he or she is not likely to be responsive after the sale either.

☞ Sending an email and getting a response about a particular product will help you learn and understand more about the seller and his or her activities, but you can do much more than this.

You may wish to see what other auctions the seller has participated. Not only will this help you determine whether to bid or not, but also you might get an invaluable clue from other previous auctions about the best selling price for the item. If the seller has sold similar items in the past, use that as a guidepost for bidding on this one. In addition, you might also find out whether the buyer is either selling other items you are interested in, in place of or this one.

Placing Your Bid

Now, you have found the perfect item to track and that it is in your affordable price range. When you are ready to jump into the eBay live auction-bidding fray, you can find the bidding form at the bottom of the auction item page (or click the Place Bid button at the top of the auction page). To fill out the bidding form and place a bid, follow these simple steps:

- Enter your maximum bid in the appropriate text box. The bid needs to be higher than the current minimum bid suggested in the box.
  You do not need to enter the dollar sign, but do use a decimal point unless you really *want* to pay $1,079.00 instead of $10.79. If you make a mistake with an incorrect decimal point, you can later retract your bid. (See Retracting a Bid," later.)

- If this is a Multiple Item auction item, enter the quantity of items that you want to buy.

- Click on the Place Bid button. Now, you have to sign into your account. When you agree to the terms and conditions, click Submit.

Bidding to the Maximum

When you make a maximum bid on the bidding form, you are actually making several small bids repeatedly, until you reach a stage where you want to stop bidding. For example, if the current bid is up to $19.99 and you put in a maximum of $50.02, your bid automatically increases incrementally, so that you stay ahead of the competition, at least until someone else's maximum bid exceeds yours.

You always bid by *proxy,* which means that your bid always rises incrementally in response to other bids.

No one will know whether you are bidding by proxy, and no one knows how high your maximum bid is either. In addition, the best part is that you can be active doing your other work while the proxy bid happens automatically in your absence. Buyers and sellers have no control over the increments (appropriately called *bid increments*) that eBay sets for them. The bid increment is the amount of money by which a bid raises, and eBay's system can work in many mysterious ways. The current maximum bid can jump up small margins, but there is also a well-conceived method to this madness! EBay uses a *bid-increment formula,* which uses the current high bid to determine how much to increase the bid increment.

Retracting a Bid

May be you like shopping in a well-stacked shopping mall. When you buy some items in a shopping mall and if you find that, you are not too keen in retaining the product with you, you can always return it to the shop. However, it is not the same on eBay.

Even if you realize that you already have an item in your home that is just like the one that you won yesterday on eBay, deciding that you do not want to go through with a confirmed transaction *is* a big deal.

Not only can it earn you some nasty and negative feedback, but it can also give you the reputation of a bad defaulter. Remember, many states consider your bid a binding contract, just like any other legal contract. You cannot simply retract your bid unless one of these three outstandingly unusual circumstances applies to your situation:

- If your bid is clearly a typographical error (you submitted a bid for $2580 when you really meant $25.80), you may retract your bid. If this occurs, you should reenter the correct bid amount immediately and rebid on that amount. You will not get any sympathy, if you try to retract a fair bid like $20.50, by saying that you meant to bid $12.55. So, always review your bid before you send it. You have tried to contact the seller to answer questions on the item, and he or she does not reply to your questions.

- When the seller substantially changes the description of an item after you place a bid (the description of the item changes from "box gloves" to "a pair of gloves," for example), you may retract your bid of the auction.

Before the 12-hour mark, a retraction removes all bids that you have placed in the auction. Mistakes or not, when you retract a bid that was placed within the last 12 hours of the listing, only the most recent bid that you made is retracted your bids placed prior to the last 12 hours are still active. Here is how to retract your bid, while the auction is still going on:

- ☞ Click on the *Services link* on the main navigation bar.

- ☞ Scroll down to the *Bidding and Buying Services* banner and click the *Retract My Bid* link.

- ☞ Read the legal clauses, scroll down the page, and enter the item number of the auction that you are retracting your bid. Then, open the dropdown list and select one of the three legitimate reasons for retracting your bid.

☞ Click the *Retract Bid* button. You receive a confirmation of your bid retraction via e-mail. Keep a copy of it until the auction is completed.

What Should I do after won the Bid?

The bidding on an auction has ended now. What will happen next? First, find out whether you have won the product. Go back to the auction page after the auction closes to see and check whether you are the winner. Go to your my eBay page (click the my eBay button at the top of any page). Scroll to the *Items I have won* section and click *Go*. This will display all the auctions you have won within the past 2 days. If more than two days have passed since the auction ended, increase the number of days in the *Show items for past days* text box and click go again.

You will also receive an email notice from eBay telling you that you have won the auction. In addition, you will most likely hear very soon from the seller as well, who will send you an email message with the details of the auction and payment information. If you do not hear from the seller, contact him or her yourself, as outlined in *Contact the Seller*.

If you do not receive a response within three days of the closing of the auction, you have the ultimate right, according to eBay rules, to back out of the auction won.

Contact the Seller

The most important part of an auction is contacting the seller. If you do that before you bid on an item, it can help you determine:

- How smoothly the buying process will go
- Will lead to you getting the goods quickly and error-free and
- Get good feedback from the seller.

If you are in good books with the buyers, you can easily build a great feedback profile

The best way to communicate with sellers is using email. Therefore, the first step in the process is to find the seller's email address. If he or she has already sent you an email in response to a question you had about the auction, you only have to respond to that email. However, if he or she has not sent an email, you will have to find the email address yourself.

To find out the e-mail address, first check the seller's *About Me* page. Click on the Search button at the top of any eBay page; then click *Find members* to display the *Find Members* page. In the *About Me* text box, type the user ID or name of the seller and click *Search*.

EBay always displays a page the member has put together about self, that includes contact and other related information. Not every eBay member has an "*About Me*" page, so it is very difficult to find an e-mail address there. However, you can always send email directly from the auction page itself. In the Seller Information section on the auction page, you will find an *Ask seller a question* link. Click on that link to see a form that lets you send an email to the seller.

Payment

Sellers generally want their payment within about a week of the auction closing, so be prompt with your payment dispatch. Paying promptly and within the suggested time ensures that the item is shipped to you quickly and that you get a positive feedback. When you have won an auction, a *Pay Now* button appears when you visit the auction page.

When you click on the Pay Now button, you get the seller's information, including mailing address, so you can send a check or money order, if you are using that payment mode. If you are going to pay by using PayPal, you can click a PayPal link and then pay using that account. For more details about payment, please see next pages.

Ask About Insure the Item

If you are buying a rare special, breakable or fragile item, you may want to insure the item during shipping against damages. Many sellers offer the insurance option upfront, but even those sellers who do not explicitly offer insurance, are often willing to insure if you specifically ask. It is best if you ask before you bid, of course, but if you are willing to pay for it, most sellers will do it for you.

As a seller, I cannot tell you how many times I have received a check or money order in the mail as an auction payment, but with no other useful information in the envelope no name, no address, no mention of the auction item or number, and nothing! It is quite difficult for even small sellers to link anonymous payments with auction items; for heavy sellers, the task can be virtually impossible.

The same goes for auction payments; you definitely want the seller to know who you are! One of the easiest ways to do this is to print out the closed item-listing page. Write your name and address at the top, and the seller will have all the information she or she needs to make sure you get what you paid for.

Never ever, demand special shipping. Do not expect same-day shipping as well. Do not expect a refund for the product just because you do not like what you get.

After Receive Your Item

When you receive the item by courier or post, open it up and check it without fail! Do not wait for a long time before you open the package and then later expect the seller to rectify a problem closed weeks ago. If everything is OK, send the seller an email about the condition of the product. (Leaving positive feedback against the buyer's name is another way to tell the seller that you are happy with your purchase.) If you do not take an immediate action on a faulty or bad product, it is yours permanently as buyer may never agree to replace the item.

Protect Yourself from Fraud and Suspect Buyers

A suspicious or fraud seller is duping one of the biggest fears of newbie users. Well, it can always happen (remember, your transaction is with an individual, not with eBay). Nevertheless, there are things you can do to minimize the risk. Read to learn some tricks that the eBay Masters use to ensure safer auction transactions.
If, after reading a seller's feedback ratings and comments, you feel unsure about buying from that seller, then never ever buy from that buyer. There are hundreds of sellers out there, and you can probably find a similar item for sale from a seller with a better feedback rating.

Trust yourself and in your intuition. If something does not smell right, there is probably a good reason. If a deal or a transaction seems too good to be true, it probably is. It is not that you cannot find some terrific deals on eBay!

Here is something nasty to watch out for hijacked eBay accounts. This happens when a hacker somehow gains access to a legitimate member's user ID and password, and then takes over that member's identity to launch a series of fraudulent auctions.

Everything looks good about that user, because the fraud is sitting behind the original user's feedback section, but the auction could be a complete sham. When you send your payment to such a buyer, it is as good as lot forever! Obviously, eBay does its best to shut down these fraudulent auctions and hijacked accounts. However, how can you identify a fraudulent/hijacked auction before you place a bid?

Here are some revealing signs of a fraudulent auction from a hijacked account:

- The auction is for a very high-priced and premium item, but the starting price or *Buy It Now* price is considerably below the typical retail price.

- Payment never includes PayPal or credit cards, instead insisting on money order, cashiers check, or Western Union cash transfer.

- The seller's feedback is primarily for buying items, not for selling.

- The seller has not completed any transactions for several months.

- While the seller's account is listed in the United States or Canada, if you contact the seller, you will find out he or she is actually in another country.

- Remember, even if the address and contact information look perfect (because they are from the original user), they will all be false and suspicious. When it comes to sending payment, the seller may ask you to mail it to somewhere else, typically in another country.

To confuse the situation, many of these scammers will send you a follow-up email that claims to be from eBay, vouching for the seller's veracity, or even offering additional insurance to cover the seller's buyers. Since eBay does not endorse individual sellers or sell such insurance, you will know instantly that this is a fraud.

If you think there is something strange about aparticular auction, refrain from bidding! Moreover, if you know something is fishy, report it to eBay immediately. If you find a seller that demands payment through Western Union or a similar cash wire transfer service (Money Gram, eGold, and so on), do not touch that auction even with a barge pole! These services will help you send money to family and friends who is the people you trust.

They are not for paying an auction item. (Note that this warning applies to Western Union cash transfers, not to Western Union Auction Payments now known as BidPay, which operates much like PayPal and is perfectly legit.)

Scammers and hackers like to receive payment through Western Union and similar cash transfer services, because it is essentially the same as wiring them physical cash, without any questions asked.
Cash wire transfers are particularly vulnerable to criminal activities, because they are not traceable, do not offer any verification procedures, and make it difficult to identify the recipient.

In other words, these services offer virtually no protection against fraud that makes them the payment method of choice for all fraudulent sellers, especially those in certain European nations. Even Western Union warns against abuse of their cash transfer service.

The safest and authentic way to pay for an auction item is by using your credit card. When you pay by credit card, the Fair Credit Billing Act protects you, by giving the right to dispute certain charges and limit your liability for unauthorized transactions up to $50.

That is right; if anything goes bad, just contact your credit card company and they will absorb all but $50 of the cost. That is a secure and safe net you do not have with any other payment method.

In addition, if you use your credit card to pay via PayPal, you have the additional coverage of PayPal's Buyer Protection Plan or (if the individual auction is not covered under the Buyer Protection Plan) the Buyer Complaint Process. PayPal investigates each claim individually, but if they agree that you have been taken for a ride, you may be eligible for a full refund.

There is another payment option you might want to consider, if you are buying at a particularly high-priced auction. An escrow service acts as a neutral (buffer) third party between you and the seller, holding your money until you receive the seller's merchandise. If you do not get the products (or the goods are unacceptable), you always get your money back; the seller is paid only when you are happy with your purchase.

Bidding Strategies

What is your plan of action or strategy for making purchases on eBay? For most people, it will be one of the following five purposes:

- Buying goods for less money: This is a money-saving strategy.
- Buying products from large selection of goods: This is a consumer-buying strategy.
- Buying goods not otherwise available conveniently: This is a timesaving strategy.
- Buying for resale: This is a profit strategy.

Thus, I do not provide any buying strategies for any particular category of merchandise, but the general strategies should work well in most cases.

Used items

These must sell at 30 percent of list price (a 70 percent discount). When anyone can buy an item new at a discount store for 60 percent of list price, used items, in excellent condition usually are not worth as much as one would think. When you have the choice of buying a new item at 60 percent of list and a used item at 40–60 percent of list, you will probably choose the new item. Realistically speaking, the market value for most used goods is normally below 40 percent of list (i.e., more than a 60 percent discount).

I will not pay more than the above guidelines. That is my buying strategy. Of course, many situations on eBay do not meet my general guidelines. Often one brand leads the field in a category, and everyone wants it.

Items with the hot selling brand name often sell on eBay for what you might pay for them in a discount store, or even higher. This does not make sense, but it happens sometimes.

Some used goods are rare, but come with very high demand. They can go at surprisingly high prices relative to their original list price. For such goods (if I needed them), I would certainly bend and relax my guidelines. Nevertheless, generally speaking, you can say that my strategy for buying on eBay is to pay less than I would pay elsewhere.

New items

These must sell at 40–55 percent of list price (i.e., a 45–60 percent discount). If you cannot get the merchandise at such low prices on eBay, you should buy it at a discount store; it is less risky. You always know the discount store, you also know where it is, and the discount store usually provides a liberal return policy. Buying from an eBay seller, you usually do not get the same assurances and promises.

Refurbished items

These are almost similar as new products, if they come in a factory-sealed box with a warranty. I will pay almost as much for these products as for new ones (i.e., discounted price) under two specific conditions. First, the refurbished items are not generally available at retail in any of the stores. If they are, the price should be significantly lower than new products.

The scarcity of factory-refurbished goods makes them almost as valuable as new ones. Second, the item is soon to become obsolete within a few years. For example, a hard drive will last for ten years in a home office. You will use it for only three or four years before you buy a bigger one. What difference does it make, if you buy a factory-refurbished one, instead of a new one?

Get a Bigger Selection

Many people live in rural or remote locations, where their local retailers do not offer the range of choices they would have in metro areas. They can find a wider range of choices on eBay. Catalog sales have thrived on this reality for over a century. Indeed, catalog sales remain high even in metro areas, where people are too busy to shop or the specialty discount store is miles away on the other side of town.

Keep in mind that a significant amount of the merchandise people sell on eBay is new. It is not all old. The main strategy here is to get a large and big selection. Low price is not as important or critical for this consumer strategy, as it is for the money-saving strategy outlined above.

Make Profit

Making profit is strictly a business strategy. For buying, you need to buy low, just as with the money-saving strategy, and sell later at a profit. For arbitrage, you need to have the confidence that you can sell immediately at a higher price.

Arbitrage

Arbitrage is buying in one market and selling immediately in another market, where the price is a little higher. In other words, if you can buy something on eBay, and sell it immediately at a higher price somewhere else, you can make a small profit.

Certainly, other online auctions do not operate as efficiently as eBay; that is, they do not have the volume to determine a stable price for a particular item. Perhaps you can engage in arbitrage between such auctions and eBay.

If you can be sure of selling something immediately for a higher price in another market, buy it on eBay, where it is likely to sell cheaper, and then resell it in the other market. This is a perfectly right business strategy that can help you make lot of money.

Arbitrage is a well-known stock market technique. It does not work as well for the more erratic and less efficient consumer products market. The transfer of stocks is immediate and instant. The cost of transfer for the traded stocks is very small. On the other hand, the transfer of products usually takes lot of time. The cost of transfer for goods involves shipping and sometimes paying sales tax and other costs.

Nonetheless, where prices are uncoordinated enough and an immediate resale is assured, you can use arbitrage to realize narrow profit margins.

Arbitrage can work in two ways for you with eBay. First, you can buy elsewhere and sell on eBay, or you can buy on eBay and sell elsewhere. The principle is simply that the resale must be certain, immediate, and profitable.

For arbitrage, the buying strategy is to buy low, but you must have a solid resale plan that you can carry out immediately.

In other words, the price you anticipate for the resale determines the upper limit for which you can buy the goods and still make a small profit on the immediate resale.

With arbitrage, you have to be extra careful. Because the profits are usually small, you cannot afford to make even a small mistake.
I might also point out that arbitrage requires large transactions, often significant amounts of capital, and extensive knowledge of the markets.

The profit is very small, so the transaction must be large to make the deal worthwhile and paying. In addition, unless you have excellent knowledge of the markets in which you deal, arbitrage is financially suicidal or disastrous.

Retail

If you can buy new products, at or below wholesale on eBay and resell at retail, you can still make a profit. However, presumably the risk of buying on eBay is higher than buying from a distributor. Thus, the price of new products on eBay will normally have to be significantly lower than wholesale to justify the risk. Thus, the profit making strategy is virtually identical to the money-saving strategy. The exception is for those goods that are in high demand that may be temporarily unavailable from distributors or manufacturers.

If you can buy such goods on eBay, even for a premium above wholesale, and resell at retail (or even above retail), you can make a profit that you otherwise would not be able to make. Here the strategy is to get the merchandise; but it is not that simple.

You still have to get the products at a low enough price to make a reasonable profit selling at retail. Nevertheless, be extra cautious. When the temporary shortage of goods passes, retail prices will fall quickly.

It is a little different strategy for used goods. Some retailers enjoy a healthy market for used products, but cannot find enough inventories to buy for resale (e.g., antique dealers). However, eBay provides them with a major source of used products that they can depend on for acquiring inventory. Here, the strategy is to build up your used inventory; but you still have to get the products at a discount deep enough to enable you to resell the goods and make a reasonable profit.

PART 3

Selling

EBay is a well-known and proven business. You must keep track of all finances; deal with suppliers, store inventory, pay taxes, make money and work hard. However, there are several differences between a conventional business and an eBay business. One of those BIG differences is the selling. The selling of products in an eBay business is much easier and less complicated than in conventional businesses.

EBay is a website that gets a huge amount of traffic every day, millions of products are bought on eBay every week and billions of dollars worth a year! More and more people are looking to buy stuff on eBay and it is extremely easy to get a membership, so you can get in on the moneymaking action!

If you have the products to sell, list them with clear pictures and descriptions and some of them will sell. The ones that do not sell...list them again! That is how simple it is to sell things on eBay, you simply have to list your product again for auction, and some of it may sell, while some of it may not.

Nevertheless, regardless of whether your products sell well or poorly, the more you list the more you will sell.

Selling your first item on eBay can be a real rush and a genuinely stressful and bitter experience. What is the right price to set? What category should it go into? As you gain more experience selling, you still run into many of these same issues.

Pricing is always a guessing game, as is category placement. However, as you sell more and more items on eBay, you run into a new issue: Where do you get more stuff to sell? Making your listings efficient and effective is not a hard task, in fact, it is very simple and that is exactly how your listings should appear simple, easy to read and full of information. Do you want to sell more? If you want to make big money, you will need to find a constant flow of products and services into the auction cart. The more you sell the more money you can make.

Prepare to Sell

Selling on eBay could be as simple or as complex as you want to make it. If you just want to place an item up for bid, you can do that with a minimum of effort and time.

You can also formalize and streamline your selling strategy and establish a business of selling items on eBay. In any case, the following sections will get you on your way. You will need a number of equipments and services to connect to and use eBay. Ideally, you should have the following:

- Computer
- Internet Connection (DSL)
- Color Printer
- Digital Camera & Scanner

Computer

What you need a computer with a stable operating system like Windows. You can buy a new desktop computer and monitor for around $500. **Y**our computer does not need to run the hottest or the fastest microprocessor nor does it need the quickest memory—it just needs the speed, memory, and storage capacity to handle the level of selling you are expecting.

Internet connection

Broadband Internet connection is almost becoming very common. It will help you upload or download data sheets and images quicker.

You can also save lot of money by using this connection; just think of those good old days when you used a snail like dial up connection! Whether you choose cable or digital subscriber, line (DSL), fast or super quick or use less popular services such as wireless broadband, is strictly a matter of cost, availability, and convenience.

Color Printer

A color inkjet printer is so inexpensive that you can probably get one bundled free with your new computer and monitor. Especially helpful are the all-in-one (MFD) products that bundle other features, such as faxing, copying, and scanning, in one unit. Flat, horizontal space always seems to be at a premium and the more you can accomplish in the least amount of space the better.

Scanner/Camera

Picture-capturing devices, such as digital cameras and a standalone scanner are as important to your eBay selling success, as the computer you use to send them to eBay servers. High quality pictures are an essential component to your e Bay listings.

In the subsequent section of this book, you will learn the simple and effective ways to make your listings attract bidders and repeat customers, step-by-step.

What to Sell

In order to make enough money on eBay, you must sell something. However, what would you sell? What type of products and services are the most profitable? Where do you get all the stuff you want to sell? You are probably clueless and confused right now and you want some good answers. Finding products and services to sell can be the hardest step of starting your eBay business. Nevertheless, if you want to be a well-known Power Seller that is one important step that you simply cannot skip!

Even though it is the hardest part of starting your eBay business, finding a supplier is relatively easy and can be done in a couple of days, if you know where to look and how to search. Even though it is easy, many people end up simply quitting eBay, because they find the task of finding a good supplier challenging and time consuming.

Selling homemade goods

If you manufacture your own items, whether you are a cook, a tailor, a bead maker or an artist, eBay can be very place to sell your products. You get to control everything about your business: the number of items you make, how much you are going to charge, and when you are going to sell them. You also get to be your own R&D (research and development) department. You can constantly be on the lookout for new ideas and new designs and be doing completed auction research to see what exactly is actually selling in your field. Then, because you are a manufacturer yourself, you can act quickly to supply what the market actually wants. It really is a win-win situation.

Remember to always sell a quality product and stand firmly behind your items. Your reputation and name is your most important asset on eBay. Do not get discouraged, if it takes some time to build up a solid customer base for your items. Just keep doing your best, creating the highest quality products, positioning them correctly, and offering fantastic customer service you will, become a famous eBay seller!

Consumer electronics

This is another large eBay category with a lot of selling potential. Practical selling tips for this category is that when you buy in wholesale lots on eBay and later resell them on eBay; buy with your user ID hidden. Many of the wholesale lot sellers hold a private auction. They offer this facility so that your user ID will not become public. There will be a tag attached against the winning buyer: "User ID kept private." This will keep you anonymous, so that no one can find out how much you make, when you break these items out into separate auctions. The Apple iPod auction was a private auction, so I could not search by the user's ID to see how much the buyer sold each of those items for and how much he or she made.

Consumer electronics encompass 19 subheadings and some of which may be new to you:

- Car electronics
- DVD players and recorders
- Digital video recorders
- Gadgets and other electronics
- GPS devices
- Home audio
- Home theater in a box
- Home theater projectors

- MP3 players and accessories
- PDAs and handheld PCs
- Portable audio
- Radios (CB, ham, and shortwave)
- Satellite, cable TV
- Satellite radio
- Telephones and pagers
- Televisions
- VCRs
- Vintage electronics
- Wholesale lots

The electronics category tends to invite many new eBay buyers. You may now want to say that you will accept bids only from eBay bidders with a 10 or more in feedback to protect yourself from non-paying bidders.

Computers

Computers and networking is another huge area of opportunity. It comes in a close third place on eBay's list. The most expensive items in this category are networking components that sell in the $10,000 range. Most of the sellers in the upper end of this category use a "BIN (Buy It Now)" option for their items. You must possess a technical knowledge of how all these computer pieces fit together, so that you can convince your buyers that you are the right person to sell them.

Shipping in this category can be very tricky, because many of the items are voluminous and large. "Local pick-up only" can be an option, or you can arrange for shipping from a local courier service. The buyer typically pays the shipping costs.

Clothing, shoes, and accessories

Clothing, shoes, and accessories are a large-volume area with tons of potential for the average eBay seller. It is very simple and straightforward. Currently, this category has is showing a $4 billion sales mark.

Another reason for increased popularity is that it is so easy to ship. Most clothing can be put right into a Priority Mail box or envelope that comes free from the U.S. post office (if you pay for Priority Mail shipping), and this makes your shipping a breeze.

Looking at the subcategories in this area is very interesting. There are huge opportunities in women's clothing, as it makes up the lion's share of this category with 38 percent market share. The next largest category is men's clothing at 16 percent.

When you list clothing, shoes, and accessories on eBay, make sure you describe each item in a comprehensive manner. Always list the size and dimensions (length from waist, length from shoulder, bust size, and so on), because sizes by manufacturer can vary a lot.

Also, list the color, type of fabric, and condition (stains, rips, and so on). Many buyers also look for items from a smoke-free environment. Make sure that you say this in your listing. Clothing is a great category in which you can find your niche, because it is readily available and easily purchased.

You can buy new clothing from department store sales, especially when items are marked down 50 percent, plus an additional percentage off. In addition, when the season is over, you can pick up clothes at great prices and hold them for the next season.

Another great idea for clothing is to sell your kids' used clothes by the lot, as they grow out of them. Some of my friends do this every season and make enough money to buy their kids new school clothes. It is a great way to recycle and save you some money. Popular children's (toddlers and infants) brands include Gap, Old Navy and Ralph Lauren.

Books, movies, and music

The books, movies, and music category is quite huge, at $3.7 billion (approximately) sales data. EBay has grouped three large top categories together to create this monster. Books, movies, and music each account for close to 33 percent of the grand total. The beauty of selling books, movies, and music is that, it is a category people like a lot. You do not have to know as much as you might to sell computers, and yet you still need to know more than you would to sell clothing.

This is a great area to choose to acquire eBay knowledge, because that is what will give you an opportunity to earn good money. Storing these items is usually easy, because of each item's small size and storage volume. **F**or additional safety, pack items in a strong Priority Mail box (which is free, if you ship Priority Mail) from the post office. For shipping details please sees next pages.

Used Products

Used products can be great sellers as well, depending on what you sell. Not every used product is a good seller and most used products are hard to sell.

Because everyone wants, NEW products, and used products usually do not come with a guarantee. You need to sell stuff that keeps its value over time. Watches, jewelry, antiques and collectibles are examples of things that keep their value very well.

Some used electronics and even clothing can also be good sellers, as long as they are relatively new. A camcorder that is only one year old and is in good condition will always sell at a fair price. If you are going to sell, used products that do not keep their value very well, you should sell relatively young products like Camcorders, DVD players, MP3 players, designer clothing, etc...

Unique items sell well because they are interesting and rare, the age sometimes adds to the value just like in collectibles.

Home and garden

Another interesting category (sales figures projected at $3.2 billion) is home and garden. This category is really a mishmash of different items, services and products. When eBay started growing in 1997 and 1998, it had to add many subcategories quickly, with some of them not making much sense to buyers.

You will find all such categories in the home and garden category. Under this main category, you find such items as bedding, building supplies, food, furniture, major appliances, tools, gardening, and even pet supplies.

This category has almost become a catchall. If eBay does not know where to categorize something, it will include them into home and garden sector. It is hard to generalize this category with tips, tricks, and insider information, because this category covers everything from building a house (including the tools you would use), to decorating it, and then to stocking your pantry and bar. Moreover, do not forget the pet supplies that everyone needs, like dog foods or ornamental plants you need for your garden.

How to find suppliers

Finding a suppler is very frustrating; it can seem like looking for a needle in a haystack if you do not know where or how to look. First, look at all those Power Sellers who are selling the same stuff that you are selling. How did they get their hands on their products? They looked for it continuously until they found it! You must understand that if you can buy a product, you can sell it for a decent profit.

You will need to look everywhere, think outside the box and get creative, if you want to sell certain specialized items. You will sometimes need to think for yourself and figure out a number of ways to get your hands on the products you want to sell on eBay. This might seem scary, but do not worry: you will get lot of information in a book that is sure to help you. Not everyone is going to agree to do business with you. Nevertheless, you must remember there are thousands of people out there that would agree to be your supplier.

The best way to find a supplier is to go to http://yellowpages.bigbook.com
or www.yellow.com or www.yell.com

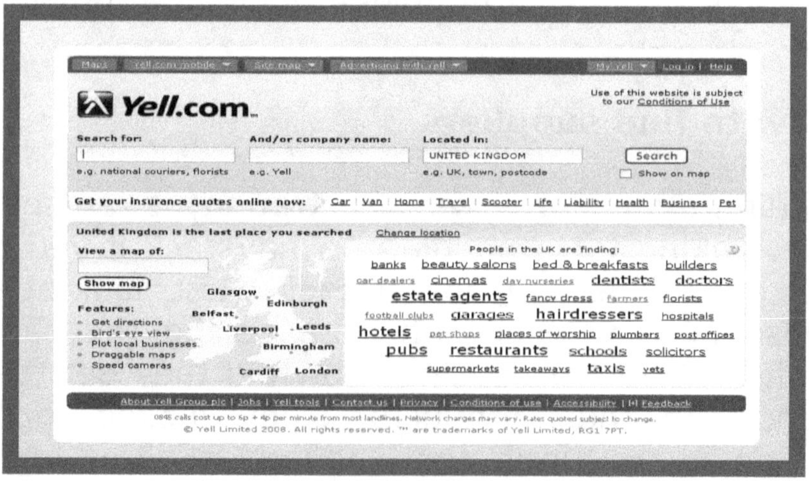

and search "wholesale" and call the suppliers by phone! Keep in mind that many suppliers will only deal with you, if you have a tax ID and when your business registered. There are no "tricks" or "secrets" to finding good suppliers, the best suppliers really can be found using yellow pages.

When looking for suppliers, you should keep this in mind - a good supplier close to home is better than a great one far away. Always find a supplier who is near to you and your home. You can also call suppliers and visit them in person!

Having a good relationship with your suppliers is an advantage to you, as you can get products at very low prices. First, register your business and get a tax ID or vendors license. This is important because most (not all) suppliers and wholesalers will not sell you their products, unless you have proper business credentials.

What is a tax ID? A tax ID allows you to purchase merchandise from a supplier without paying taxes and allows you to collect taxes when you sell the merchandise you bought.
You do not have to get a tax ID, but you need it to buy products without any problems.

Most suppliers want you order a minimum order quantity of products, which means if you want to buy from them, you must buy the minimum amount required, otherwise they will not sell you anything. So, even when you have your business registered and have a tax ID, it does not necessarily mean you will be able to buy the products you want.

If you do not want to register your business or cannot afford the minimum order restriction, there are still many ways for you to sell the things on eBay. Get to know someone that already sells the products on eBay. This is all about partnerships, you need a good partner that owns or runs a store selling the products you are also looking to sell on eBay.

Your main goal is to purchase the products from a supplier through your partner's business, leaving your partner with a share in your profits. If that sound complicated, let me break it down: Find a store that already sells the products you want to sell on eBay. Talk to the owner and tell him or her about your plan. Tell him or her that you are looking for a business partner who can supply you with a large quantity of a certain product.
Tell your future partner that all he/she would have to do is help you in selling some products and you will pay him or her chunk of the profits.

Now, when you are talking to your future partner, make sure you make your business proposition cajoling and attractive.

Tell him/her how much extra income this partnership can make and tell him/her that by ordering an extra amount of products every month might help make more money.

Do not talk so much about what you want; instead, focus on what he/she will gain by being your supplier/partner. After you have found a person that can supply you with the products, all you have to do is tell them the exact volume of products you need and your new partner may simply call his/her supplier and order those products for you. With this, you will be able to take the best advantage of your partner's bulk discounts and order small quantities of products at large quantity discounts.

Now what you may ask is; does anyone actually do this? Do people actually become Power Sellers using the method just mentioned above? Yes! Many sellers use this method to sell expensive clocks and watches on eBay. Most watch companies will accept only minimum orders and sell only to authorized dealers.
To become an authorized dealer is very hard and most stores do not qualify to become one.

The only advantages of using the above method are- you do not need to get a tax ID and you will be able to buy small quantities at bulk discounts.

How can you make the products come to your home? By running ads in newspapers and posting in internet forums, you can say something like "I will buy your products". If you are going to use this method, you will need to pick a product that retains its value very well, because you will be buying mostly used and second hand products. Therefore, used shoes or electronics will not work (unless they are collectable and antique). If you are going to use this method, you should buy things like jewelry and watches, antiques and other things that can get better and valued with age.

Manufacturers' goods

There are plenty of manufacturers of products in every city in the United States and abroad. Nearly every manufacturer would love to find a non-traditional selling channel to sell returned and slow selling products. *Non-traditional* is a type of product that will not compete with its existing channels of distribution. Check the Yellow Pages in your city for any manufacturing company that can provide the service to you.

Becoming a Supplier

If you do not have enough money of your own to start selling products, you can always use other people's money or other people's products. You will be buying large quantities of products from suppliers and you do not need to have any money to start buying such products.

First, you will need to decide the type of products you want to sell. You can supply other sellers with products and services foe reselling. Alternatively, you can also sell business supplies like tape, bubble wrap, labels, pens, paper or even computers. When you decide about the products, the next step is finding a regular supplier. Once again, you should look for a supplier in your city, so you can visit them in person and discuss about the business venture.

Once you find a supplier and work out things like prices, delivery time, payment etc, list the products up for pending auction. Most suppliers have a minimum order quantity prescribed for every buyer (30 items, 40 items, 2,000 etc.), so you will need to make sure you sell the minimum amount required in order to get the best discount from your supplier.

If the minimum order, quantity placed by you is 1,000 items make sure you sell most of them because, the supplier will not be willing to deal with you in future if you do not provide the best results. You may also get a bunch of negative feedback from your customers. Once you sell the products, collect the money from your customers, approach your supplier, pay him/her for the products, and pocket your profits.

After you pay your supplier, simply ship the products to your customers and repeat the process until you are rich with your profits! What you are doing is getting people to pay YOU for products you actually do not own. Now let us get to the money part.

Let us say the supplier you have found has a minimum order quantity (MOQ) of 1,000 items and each item costs $10. That means the supplier has a minimum order of $10,000. What you will need to do is sell at least 1,000 items if you want to make good profits. Alternatively, you can even sell products in lots of 25, 30, 50, 100 etc.

Since you are buying each item at $10, you should sell it for at *least* $12-$13 in order to make a good profit. Why would people buy from you at $13 an item when they can buy directly from a supplier for $10 an item?

Because, the MOQ here is only 25 items, as opposed to 1,000 items purchased from a supplier.

Most sellers cannot afford to pay $10,000 for a minimum order, and that is why they will come to you for products. So, how much money will you be able to make with this transaction? Well, if you sell 1,000 items at $13 each, you will make $3,000 in profit.

Again, it will take you only a couple of transactions to sell 100 items, because you will not be selling each item on an individual basis. Now, another concern will be the shipment of the actual products to their respective buyers.

Yes! Because it does cost a lot to ship a big order, and NO because the supplier will most likely receive a large shipping discount, because he/she may ship orders to all corners of the world on a daily basis, and because the shipping cost is already included in the cost of each item.

Therefore, when you decide to list wholesale lots, you can provide free shipping on each product, and with this, you can attract a lot of attention. The great thing about being a supplier is that when you provide good service to your customers, most of them will come back and buy from you repeatedly.

Remember, it will only take you a couple of transactions to sell 1000 items, because you are selling on a bulk basis. You are not selling something that you own and you do not need to buy anything at all. All you need is 10 or less sales on eBay to make $3000 and you do not have to invest any money here! Something very important that you should know here is that you do not have to sell things that come from an actual wholesale supplier. The stuff you sell may also come from a liquidator.

A liquidator is someone who buys overruns from big retailers (Sears, Wal-Mart etc.) at a fraction of the wholesale price for the products. Sometimes, big stores cannot sell everything they have in stock. The products and services they could not sell needs to be disposed of as soon as possible to make room for new products. This is where liquidation companies come in and buy the overruns products at a fraction of the wholesale price.

When a liquidation company buys a couple of truckloads full of overruns, the next thing it must do is sell these overruns as soon as possible to make room for more overruns. Since the liquidator must get rid of the quickly, the products are sold at extremely cheap prices and always in bulk quantities.

Liquidation companies are always looking to get rid of the stock as soon as possible and that is where you come in to help by offering to sell their stock. The greatest thing about selling things from a liquidator is that their prices are usually very low!

Since the liquidator sells the products at well below wholesale prices, it gives you a lot of room for making profit. You can use OPP and OPM to sell all kinds of stock. You can even sell houses, boats, or jewelry collections. Just look in the for sale listings of your local newspaper and look at all of the great products for sale that may sell on eBay. Call the owners of the items advertised in the newspaper and offer to sell the products for them. Looking for products in newspapers is great because people who read newspapers probably know nothing about eBay and are desperate to get rid of the products they are advertising. They are also the ones that are willing to lower the price. It is great because the lower the price they are willing to let the item go for the more profit you can make by selling the product.

As you can see, the place you source your products from, does not need to be a wholesaler and the products do not have to be brand new as well.

The most important thing to remember:

- OPP Other Peoples Products and
- OPM Other People's Money

ORDER SAMPLES

Many people that are starting out on eBay make the mistake of placing a big order before actually seeing what they are actually ordering. By ordering samples, you will be able see the quality of the products but also the service, communication and legitimacy of the company you are ordering. There are many scammers out there, especially on the internet. Some websites may have clear pictures of the products they are selling, but do not make the mistake of assuming that the pictures on their website are actual pictures of the products you are ordering.

If you are thinking of selling designer clothing on eBay, be extra careful, when ordering your supplies from the internet. There is fake (counterfeit) clothing sold on the internet. The pictures on the supplier's website may look real, but that does not mean they will be sending you the products given in the picture. Once again, always order samples! If you do not, you may be in for a nasty surprise.

If the person you are buying from will not allow you to order a sample, simply stop communicating with that person, before they can exploit you.

Here are some B2B websites and other places where you can find good products to sell:

- www.yell.com,
- http://yellowpages.bigbook.com
- www.yellow.com

Contacting them is the best way to find suppliers in your area and you can do it over the internet! These web sites will help you find suppliers in your area, their addresses and phone numbers and their location. When searching for them, try important key words like overstock, closeout, liquidation, salvage, auction, surplus, refurbished, wholesale, supplier and other similar words.

For more details about website directories, please see the next part. Using these websites, you will be able to find suppliers who can supply hundreds of thousands of products. These websites provide a list of wholesale sellers who can provide all their information about thousands of products.

Start to Sell Your Items

Remember that before you can list an item for sale, you will need to be a registered eBay user. It also helps to have your credit card on record, so that you can pay the fees incurred towards using the service. Listing an item for sale on eBay is simple; all you have to do is work through the following series of steps. This is very easy and simple!

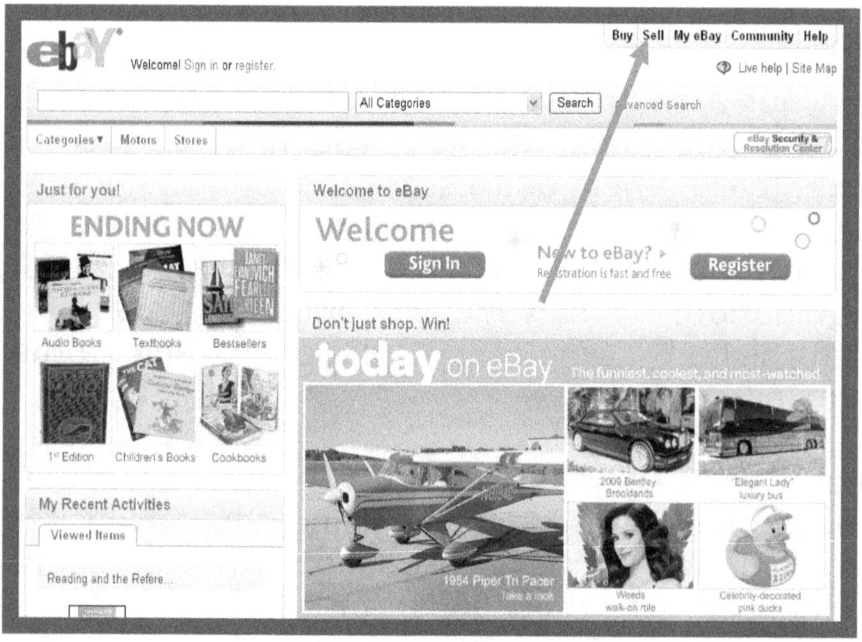

All you have to do is click the *Sell* link in the eBay-Navigation Toolbar. EBay now displays the Sell hub, as shown in the following figure. This is where you start creating your listing; click the *Sell Your Item* button to proceed

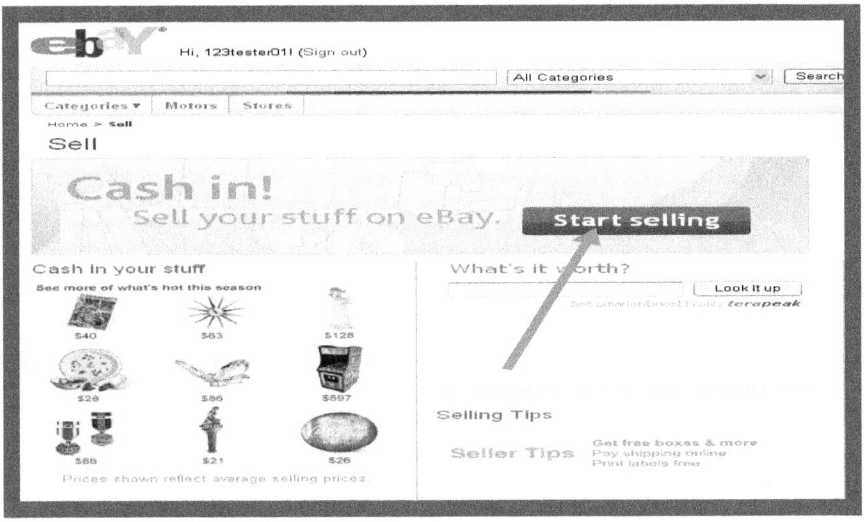

The next page will help you select the best selling category section for your item. There are two ways to select a category.

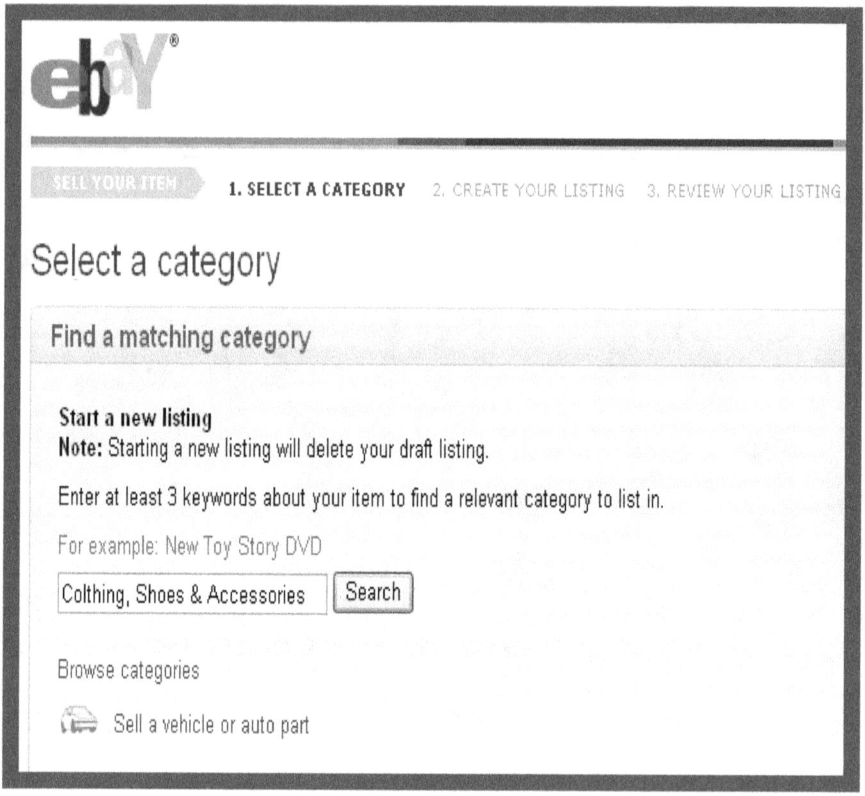

You can browse through all of eBay's available categories until you find the one you want, or you can let eBay suggest a category for you. We will examine the first method first. **T**o browse through all available categories, click the *Browse Category Directory* link. This displays an expanding hierarchical tree for all of eBay's major categories. Start by selecting a major category from the first category list, and then select a subcategory from the next list, then a further subcategory from the succeeding list, and so on. Continue selecting subcategories until there are not any more subcategories to select. A faster and quicker way to select a category is to search for it. All you have to do is enter a few descriptive keywords into the enter words about your item, to find a category for it box, and then click the *Search* button. EBay now displays the *Choose a Category* page, and you can select the best category from this list and click the Continue button.

Find Your Product

Depending on the type of item you are selling, you may now see a *Find Your Product* window, which prompts you to enter any identifying information about your item. You will see this window, when you are selling certain types of commonly sold products, such as books, CDs, DVDs, video games, digital cameras, and the others.

When you enter the UPC bar code, ISBN number, model number or similar identifier for your item, eBay automatically creates your item listing with pre-filled item information. We will discuss the pre-filled option in the *"Selling Commonly Sold Items with Pre-Filled Item Information"* section, later in this chapter. For now, let us assume you are listing the standard ways, if you see the *Find Your Product* Window; click the *Continue without Link* to bypass the pre-filled information feature. **T**he next page you see is the *Describe Your Item* page, as shown in the figure. You will use this page to enter the bulk of the information about the item you are selling. You start out by entering a title for your item; you can enter up to 55 characters. You can also enter a subtitle for your item (in the Subtitle box), although this will cost you an extra $0.50.

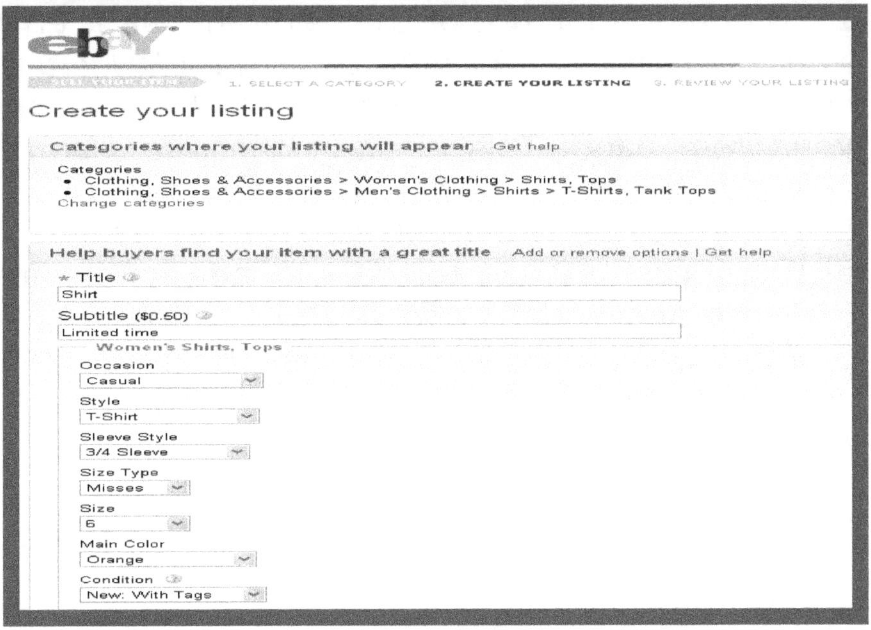
1. SELECT A CATEGORY
2. CREATE YOUR LISTING
3. REVIEW YOUR LISTING
Create your listing
Categories where your listing will appear
Get help
Categories
Clothing, Shoes & Accessories > Women's Clothing > Shirts, Tops
Clothing, Shoes & Accessories > Men's Clothing > Shirts > T-Shirts, Tank Tops
Change categories
Help buyers find your item with a great title
Add or remove options | Get help
Title
Shirt
Subtitle ($0.50)
Limited time
Women's Shirts, Tops
Occasion
Casual
Style
T-Shirt
Sleeve Style
3/4 Sleeve
Size Type
Misses
Size
6
Main Color
Orange
Condition
New: With Tags

If you have a picture of the item and want eBay to host the picture for you, click the *Add Pictures* button in the *Pictures* section of the *Describe your item* page. This displays the *Add Pictures* window, as shown in the figure. You can include just one picture with your listing free; additional pictures cost $0.15 apiece. To add a picture, click the appropriate *Add Pictures* button. When prompted, browse your hard disk for the picture, and then click *Open* to add the picture to the *Add Pictures* window.

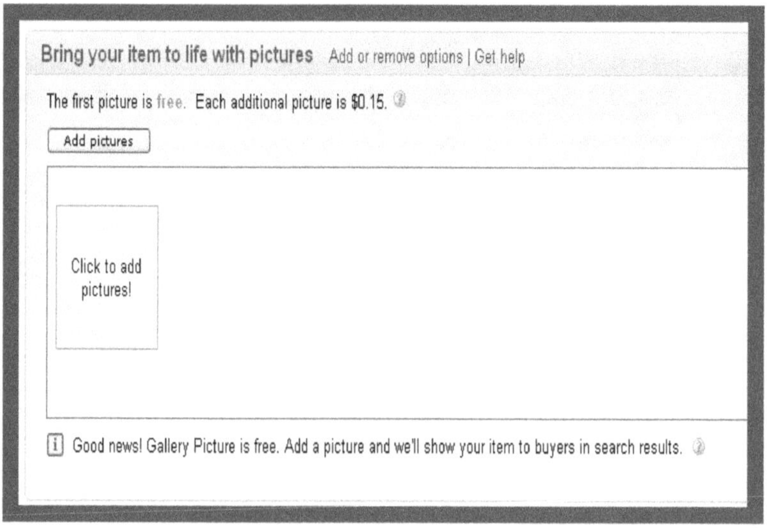

The *Add Pictures* window offers some basic picture editing functions, which is useful and beneficial, if your photos are not quite clear and sharp. Once you select a picture, you can rotate it; crop it; or even click the *Auto Fix* button to perform a quick and automatic touchup; or click the *Advanced Edit* button to adjust brightness and contrast.

The Standard option for including picture is free and gives you a 400 x 400-pixel picture at the bottom of your listing. The Supersize Pictures option costs $0.75, but lets you include a larger picture (up to 800 x 800 pixels) with a smaller click-to-enlarge thumbnail.

The *Picture Show* option (free) lets you display multiple photos in a slideshow player. In addition, the *Picture Pack* option provides a combination of Gallery, Supersize, and Picture Show features for up to six pictures, for a single $1.00 price. When you finish editing and selecting images, click the *Upload Pictures* button. This way you can upload selected photos from your hard disk to the eBay server.

Next stage is the *Item Description* box, as shown in the figure. This is where you enter a description of any length of the item.

Provide as much information and detail as you feel appropriate, and then format the text as you like. (You can even enter raw HTML code, by clicking the View HTML link.) Preview your formatted description by clicking the *Preview Description* button.

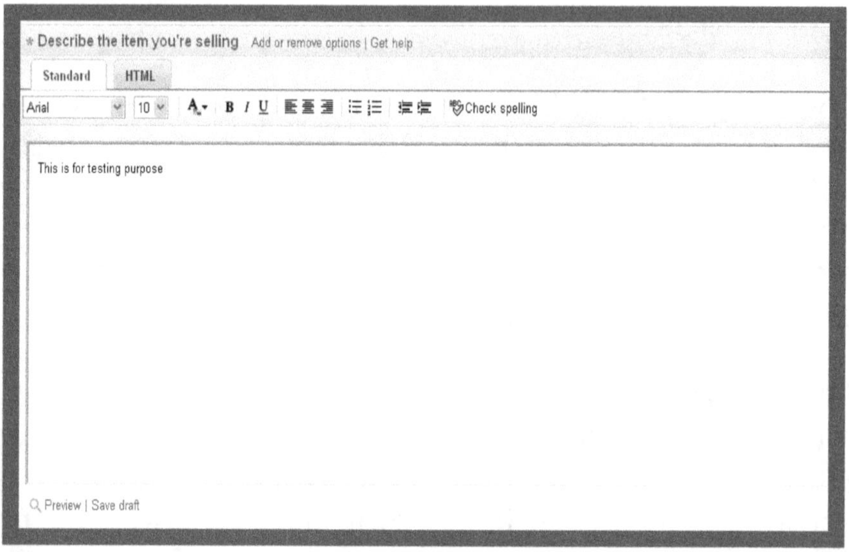

EBay lets you create fancy listings without the need for additional listing creation software for a paltry $0.10 per listing. It is a two-part process; you start by selecting a theme, and then choose the kind of picture layout you want. The themes are simple, with different underlying borders and colors. The layouts always affect the placement of your pictures on the left, right, top, or bottom. When you select a layout, you can preview it in a thumbnail to the right of the *Theme* list.

To display a hit counter at the bottom of your listing, pull down the *Visitor Counter* list and select either *Andale Style or Green LED*. If you do not want to display a counter, select the blank option from the list.

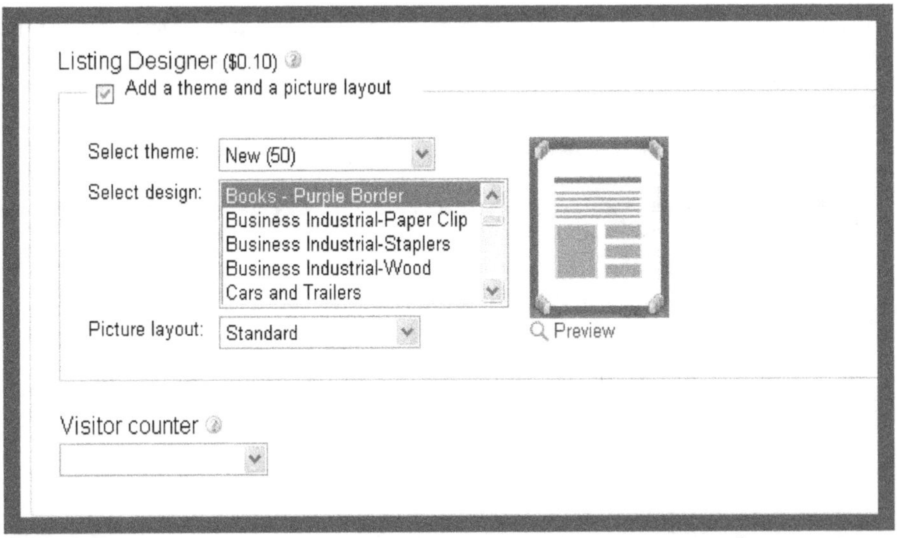

Next, you need to determine the type of auction to launch and for how long. To select the auction type, pull down the first list as shown in the figure. You can choose from several types of selling formats, although options are displayed for all users. Most users will choose the *Online Auction* option.

Now you have to set the starting (initial bid) price for your auction, as well as enter the reserve price or *Buy It Now* price (if you choose to use these options).

For a normal, non-reserve, non-BIN (Buy it Now) auction, just enter a single price into the *Starting Price* box. Enter the quantity you have to sell (typically "1"), and then pull down the *Duration* list and select how long you want your auction to run. The typical auction runs seven days, although you can choose from 1-, 3-, 5-, 7-, or 10-day auctions. (A 10-day auction costs $0.40 extra.)

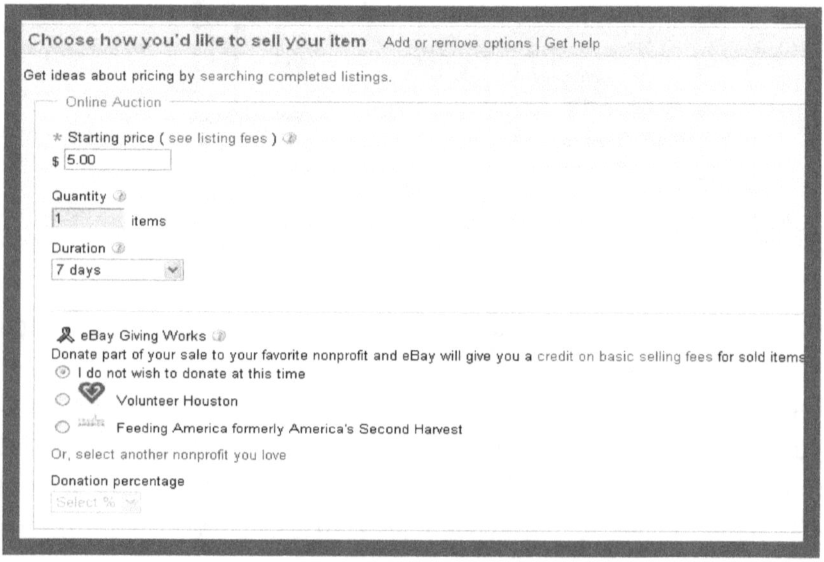

Finally, you can choose to donate some of your auction proceeds to a designated non-profit organization. Select the non-profit you want and the percent you want to donate and then continue scrolling down the page.

The next section, shown in the figure on the next page, is where you select the payment options that you accept. You can opt for payment by PayPal, Money Order/Cashier's Check, Personal Check, or Other. (If you choose the other option, be sure to describe your payment options in the *Description* section of your item listing.)

If you accept PayPal payments, you will need to enter your email address into the *"Email Address for receiving Payment"* box. (PayPal identifies members by their email addresses.) With this information entered, eBay can route any credit card payments to the correct PayPal account.

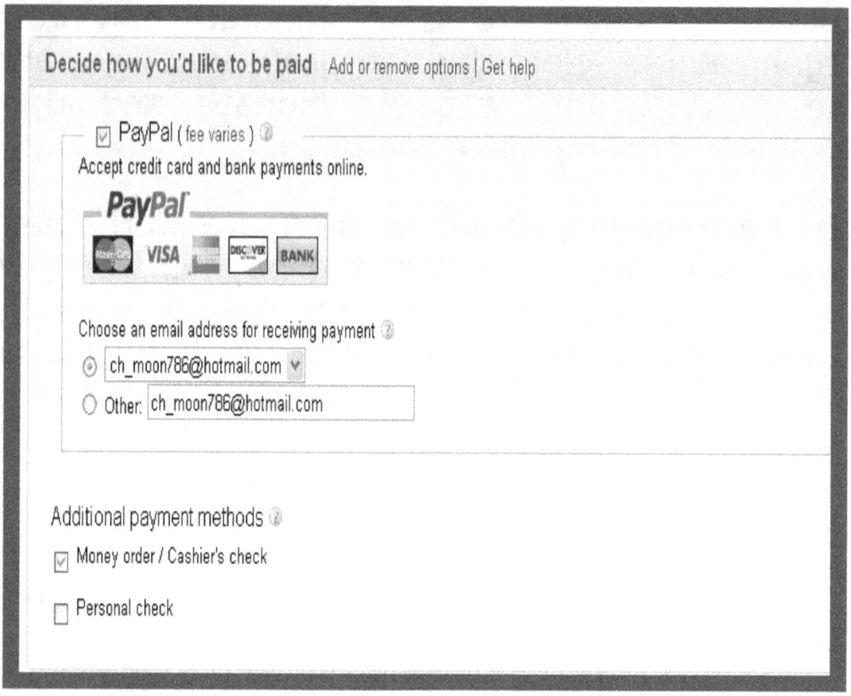
Decide how you'd like to be paid
Add or remove options | Get help
PayPal (fee varies)
Accept credit card and bank payments online.
PayPal
VISA
BANK
Choose an email address for receiving payment
ch_moon786@hotmail.com
Other: ch_moon786@hotmail.com
Additional payment methods
Money order / Cashier's check
Personal check

Next on the page is the *Shipping* section as shown in the figure. If you plan to offer shipping outside the U.S., pull down the *International Shipping Services* list, select a shipper, and (if necessary) enter the shipping charge into the adjacent box. Ensure that you check those regions to which you are ready to ship, in the *Shipping Locations* section. Finally, if you have multiple items for sale and are willing to offer a shipping discount to anyone purchasing more than one item, check the *Shipping Discount* box. (For more details, please shipping & insurance next pages.)

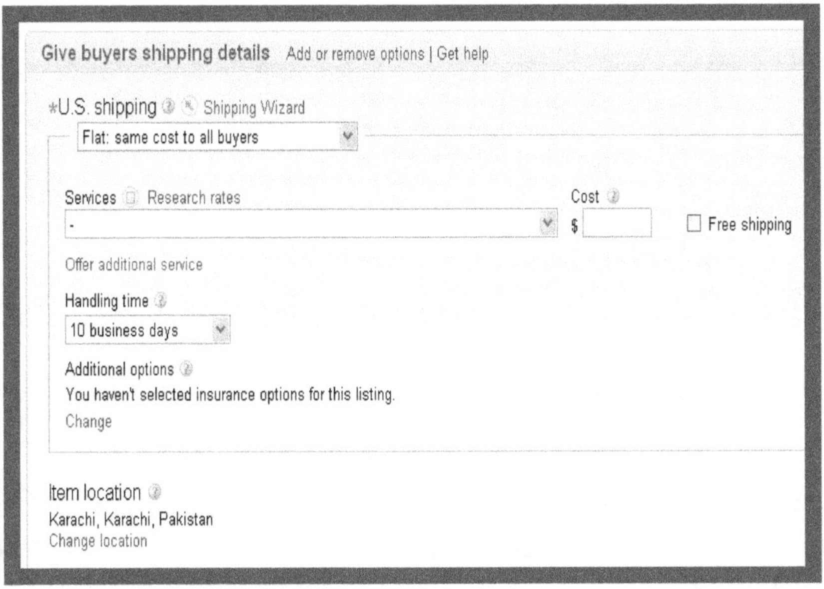

Finally, you will reach the bottom of the *Describe Your Item* page, as shown in the figure. If you are ready to accept returns from your customers, check the *Returns Accepted* box, then enter/select the appropriate information regarding your returns policy. When you finish, double-check your entries on the page and click the *Continue* button.

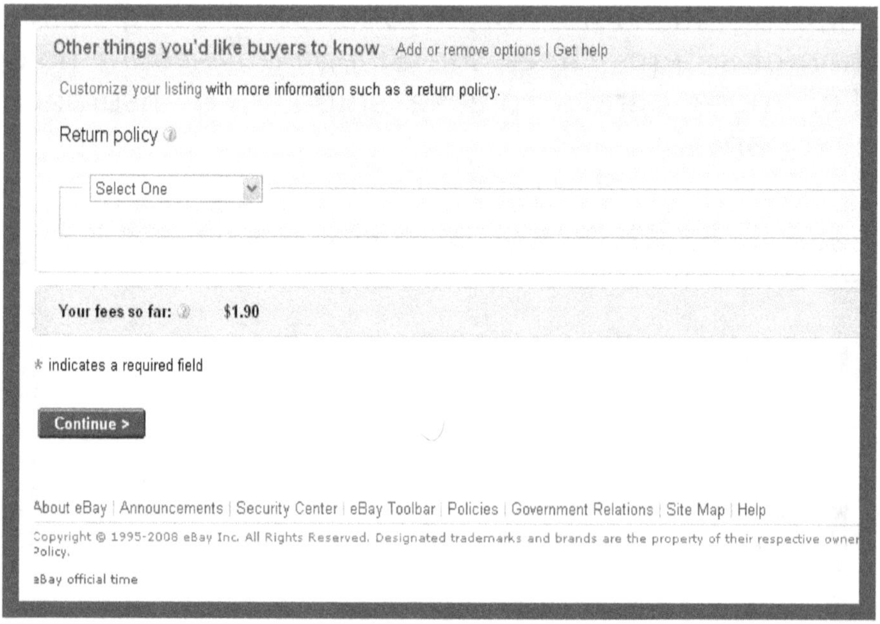

The next page offers you the opportunity to enhance your auction listing in various ways, and then to review the sales results. These facilities cost an extra charge; choose too many of them and you will wipe out your potential profit.

When you finish your work, eBay displays the *Congratulations* page. This page confirms your listing and presents you with important details about your auction, including your item listing's URL, in case you want to publicize your auction elsewhere on the Internet. After you reach the *Congratulations* screen, your completed listing should appear immediately on the eBay website, although it might take a few hours to get a complete live listing in the appropriate category.

Sell Something without Buying

Do you have a service to offer or an opinion that someone would pay for?

You can list your services or expert opinions for sale on eBay using your own catchy headline as the auction listing title. In the listing, write a short summary of the information or service you are offering and your own personal review/endorsement.

You could do a *Buy It Now* auction, or just start the bidding at some start figure. When the auction ends and the buyer pay you, all you need to do is email your information as an attachment or provide your service! You will not face packaging hassles or shipping troubles here.

Selling Commonly Sold Items

Choose a *Listing Option* page. If you recall, you have two options to choose from, listing the standard way or listing with pre-filled item information. Let us discuss that pre-filled option now.

EBay has created a huge database of commonly sold products like books, audio books, audiocassettes, CDs, DVDs, and various consumer electronics products. If you are selling one of these items, you can have eBay create your item description for you, using the information stored in its database and add a stock photo of the item, as well. All you have to do is tell eBay what you are selling, and eBay will do the hard work for you.

It all starts when you choose a product category for your listing. If the item you are selling is part of eBay's pre-filled information database, you will see a *Find Your Product* window.

You can enter identifying information, which could be the item's model number, title, artist, director, and author, UPC, or ISBN code. Enter the appropriate information, and then click the Search button. All items matching your search will fill up your search box; check your particular item, then click the *Save Selection* button.

EBay now moves to a standard *Describe Your Item* page, but with the item title and other details already entered. You will want to review the pre-filled information to make sure it is correct and accurate; you can choose not to include this information, by un-checking the Include *the Product Information* in *My Listing* option.

You will also note that eBay adds its database information outside the standard item description area, which means you, can still enter your item description into the *Description box*, if you want. From here, you should continue with the balance of the item listing process, as normal.

Setting up eBay Store

An eBay store is basically a set of special pages on eBay that show all the items a seller has for sale, including *Buy-it-now* items that don't show up in an auction search. If you have an eBay store, a red price tag icon appears next to your user ID. Potential buyers can click on this icon to go directly to your eBay store.

Listing items in a store is lot cheaper than listing them at auction, although you pay a flat monthly rate to own the store. A basic store costs $15.95 per month.

The process of listing items in a store is the same as it is to list at auction, except that you listing items in a store are cheaper than listing them at auction, although you pay a flat monthly rate to have the store. A basic store costs $15.95 per month.

The process of listing items in a store is the same as it is to list at auction, except that you choose a different selling format and click the store with a fixed price radio button. Items can stay in your store for 30 days, 60 days, 90 days, or GUC (good until cancelled). When a buyer does a title search, your auction item matching that title will come up for the buyer to view. That same search, however, will not bring up store items, unless there are less than an eBay-specified number (this number changes) up for sale at auction.

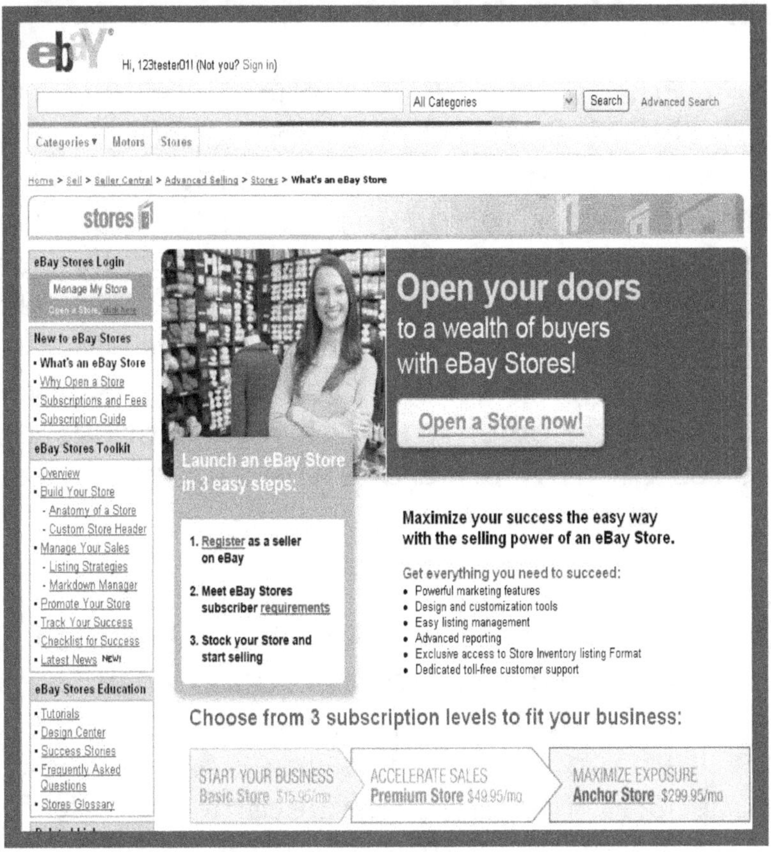

You can open your store by visiting:

http://pages.ebay.com/storefronts/start.html

Selling at Fixed Price

EBay's *Buy It Now* (BIN) option lets you add a fixed-price buying option to your auction listings. The way BIN works is quite simple; you just name a fixed price for your item; if a user bids on that price, the auction is automatically closed and that user will be the high bidder. Note, however, that the BIN price is active only until when someone places a bid. If the first bidder places a bid lower than the BIN price, eBay removes the BIN price and the auction proceeds normally later.

Why would you add the BIN feature to your auction? I find that many sellers who use BIN are retailers with a large quantity of similar inventory. That is, they are likely to place the same item up for auction week after week; in this scenario, the BIN price becomes the de facto retail price of the item. You might also want to consider BIN around the Christmas holiday, when buyers do not always want to wait for seven days to see whether they have won an item or not; desperate and hurrying Christmas shoppers will sometimes pay a premium to get something, which is where BIN comes in handy.

You can activate BIN, when you are creating your item listing for selling, in the *Selling Format* section of the *Describe* page. Just enter your BIN price into the *Buy It Now Price* box.

In addition, remember: Your BIN price should be higher than your *Starting Price.* You also have to pay eBay for each item you list and each item you sell, just as in a normal auction. The difference is that you are not listing for a (relatively short) auction, but you are listing for longer-term inventory. While eBay provides a detailed fee schedule, it pretty much boils down to paying $0.02 per month for each item listed in your eBay Store. If you list an item for 60 days, you pay $0.04; if you list an item for 90 days, you pay $0.06. Moreover, for every item you sell in your eBay Store, eBay charges a final value fee.

EBay Stores also offers a full assortment of listing upgrades, just like the ones you can use in regular eBay auctions. You can also offer multiples of the same items in Dutch auction format.

Payment Methods

Several payment options are available to sellers on eBay, but the seller has the right to refuse some forms of payment. Usually, the accepted forms of payment will be in the item's description or in the *Shipping and Payment Details* area just below the item description. The following forms of payment are available to you:

- Credit Card
- PayPal
- Money Order
- Personal Check

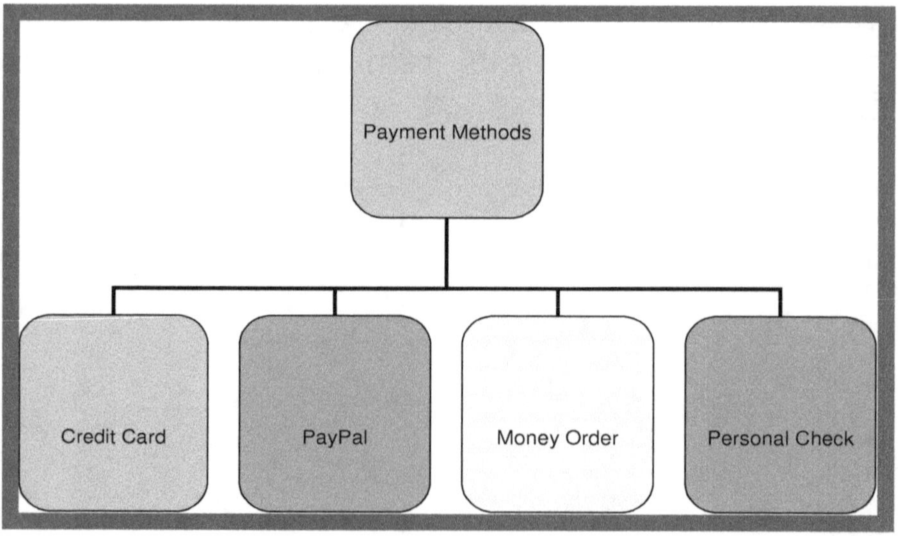

Credit card

Paying with a credit card is a favorite payment option with all buyers. I like paying with credit cards because credit cards are fast and efficient. In addition, using a credit card offers you buyer protection, if you are not completely satisfied with the transaction.

Sometimes, sellers use a friend's firm to run credit card payments for eBay auctions.

PayPal

You can pay for your eBay purchases through PayPal. Owned by eBay, PayPal is the largest Internet-wide payment network. Sellers who accept PayPal have a special icon in the *Seller Information* box (as well as a large PayPal logo in the *Payment Methods* area below the description) and accept American Express, Visa, MasterCard, and Discover, as well as electronic checks and debits. This integrated service helps buyers to buy products with one single mouse click.

After you register with PayPal service to pay for an item, PayPal debits your credit card or your bank checking account (or your PayPal account if you have earned some money from sales) and sends the payment to the seller's account.

PayPal does not charge buyers to use the service. Buyers can use PayPal to pay any seller within & outside the United States. For more details, check out the PayPal Web site (www.paypal.com).

Money Order

My second-favorite method of payment and the most popular at eBay is the money order. Sellers love money orders because they do not have to wait for a check to clear.

Personal Check

Many buyers still prefer to pay for their purchases, via personal check. Buyers like paying by check because it is convenient, and checks can be tracked (or even canceled), if problems arise with the seller.

Sellers always dislike personal checks, because they do not provide them instant money. When you deposit a check in your bank, you are not depositing cash. Check payments can take some time, typically 10 business days or more. If you ship an item on immediate receipt of a personal check and then a week later you get a notice from your bank that the check has bounced, you deserve to lose every single penny of that transaction.

Eager shippers and personal checks just do not mix nor will gel and you learn from your mistake in the future.

Because, some buyers still prefer paying by check, you should probably be prepared to handle this payment method. When you receive a check, deposit it as soon as possible with your bank, but do not ship the item until you confirm the payment. Wait until the check clears the bank (two weeks if you want to be safe longer for checks on non-U.S. banks), before you ship the item. If, after that period, the check has not bounced, it is okay to proceed with shipment.

If you have an incidence of bounced check, hope not lost yet. The first thing to do is get in touch with your bank and asks them to resubmit the check in question. Maybe the buyer was just temporarily out of funds. Maybe the bank made a mistake. Whatever the case is, sometimes bounced checks "un-bounce" when you resubmit them. Whether you resubmit the check or not, you should definitely email the buyer and let him know what happened. At the very least, you will want the buyer to reimburse you for any bad check fees, your bank charged you. The buyer might also be able to provide another form of payment to get things moving again.

Escrow service

Even though most sales at eBay are for buying items that cost $100 or less, using an escrow service comes in handy on many occasions — like when you buy a big-ticket item or something extremely rare. Escrow is a service that allows a buyer and seller to protect a transaction by placing the money in the hands of a neutral third party, until a specified set of conditions are met.

Sellers note in their item descriptions if they are willing to accept escrow. If you are nervous about sending a lot of money to someone you do not really know, consider using an escrow company.

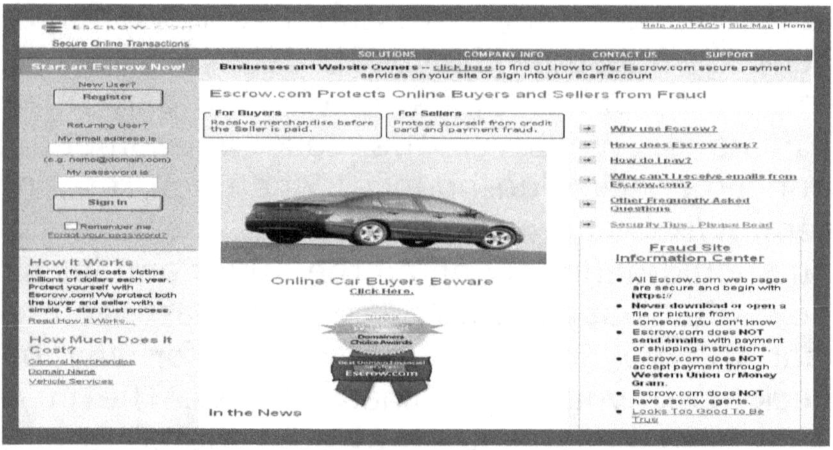

EBay has a partnership with Escrow.com that handles eBay auction-escrow sales in Canada and the United States. After an auction closes, the buyer sends the payment to the escrow company. After the escrow company receives the money, it e-mails the seller to ship the merchandise. After the buyer receives the item, he or she has an agreed-on period (normally two business days) to check it over for quality and let the escrow service know that the product is good and satisfactory. If everything is okay, the escrow service sends the payment to the seller.

If the buyer is unhappy with the item, he or she must ship it back to the seller. When the escrow service receives word from the seller about the returned item, the service returns the payment to the buyer (minus the escrow company's handling fee). Before you start an escrow transaction, make sure that you and the seller agree on these terms.

Packaging

Packing your item correctly and safely can be one of the most important parts of your eBay business. Many people starting out on selling have no idea how to package items. They just put them in any old box, slap some tape on and hope it arrives on time in a perfect condition.

In many cases, buyers may receive the product in a bad or damaged state, which will eventually result in returns and unsatisfied customers. The main goal is to pack the item correctly which will make your customer happy and make them want to buy from you again.

Adopt following steps for packaging:

Whenever possible, use a new and tough box. The more times a box is used, the more it loses its original protective qualities, so a previously used box may not adequately protect your shipment.
If you must reuse a box, make sure it is rigid and in excellent condition with no punctures, tears, rips, or corner damage, and that all flaps are intact. Remove any labels and all other shipment markings from the box.

Choose a box strength that is suitable for the contents you are shipping. Never exceed the maximum gross weight for the box (which is usually on the Box Maker's Certificate on the box's bottom flap).

It is very important that you cushion and protect the contents of your package properly. Please be sure that you wrap each item separately.

Fragile articles need both suitable separation from each other, and clearance from the corners and sides of the box. Surround each item with at least two inches (five cm) of cushioning and place the product at least two inches (five cm) away from the walls of the box. This will protect your items from product against damage and later shield them from the shock and vibration. Please use proper cushioning material, combined with a strong outer container, to protect your shipment fully. Make sure you use enough cushioning material to ensure that the contents do not move, when someone shakes the container. Improper cushioning material includes clothing, blankets, and pillows.
Instead, please use the materials listed below to cushion and protect your shipment:

- Select appropriate density of foam to meet packaging needs, which can range from void-fill applications to high-performance cushioning.

- Used primarily as a void-fill material for light-to-medium weight, non-fragile items and items that are suitable for such packing materials·

- Proper closure of your container is just as important as proper cushioning for the safety and security of your shipment.

- To close a box securely, do not use masking tape, cellophane tape, duct tape, string, or paper over-wrap.

- For fast and efficient delivery, keep in mind when labeling your package with your and buyer's address. Always include the recipient's postal code with the complete street address. For international shipments, include a contact name, telephone number, and postal code.

Shipping Container

After you assemble the packaging, all you need to do is to place your item in a box and seal it up. However, the consequences of choosing the wrong container can be both disastrous and unnecessarily expensive. First, you have to decide whether to use a box or an envelope. If you have a very large item to ship, the choice is easy. Consider the nature of the product before you choose the packaging materials. If the item can bend or break, choose a box; if not, an envelope is probably a safe choice.

Whatever you choose, pick a container that is large enough to hold your item without the need to force it in or bend it in an inappropriate fashion. Also, make sure that the box has enough extra room to insert cushioning material. On the other hand, the container should not be so big as to leave room for the item to bounce and dance around. In addition, you always pay for size and for weight of the package. You do not want to pay to ship anything bigger or heavier than it needs to be.

If you are shipping your product in an envelope, consider using a bubble-pack envelope or reinforcing the envelope with pieces of cardboard. This is especially vital when you do not want your product container bent or folded.

If you are shipping in a box, make sure that it is made of heavy, corrugated cardboard and has its flaps intact. Thinner boxes such as shoeboxes or gift boxes simply are not strong enough for rugged shipping. When packing a box, never exceed the maximum gross weight for the box, which is usually on the bottom flap.

Here are more ideas on packaging. You can take a larger box and cut it down. That means cutting through each corner of the box to make it shorter, and then cutting off the ends of the flaps accordingly.

Sometimes, it is very difficult to fold un-scored flaps, so you may want to make your own by slicing a knife (shallowly) where you want to bend the box closed.

Second, you can combine two smaller boxes. If your box is 16 inches long and your item is 20 inches, just take two boxes and insert the open end of one inside the open end of the other. You will need to use sufficient packing tape to keep the boxes from sliding apart, but you will have created a box custom-sized for the item you are shipping.

Insurance

Should you add insurance when you ship your items? The really depends on what you sell, how much it is worth and how well does your item ship.

If you sell items that rarely are damaged in shipping and are in the small price range, adding insurance may not be really worth it. The extra amount you pay for insurance may outweigh the cost, if you have a lost or damaged item.

Many sellers will only add insurance, if the customer specifically asks for it. Does this mean that if their item arrives damaged, then it is tough luck for them because they did not ask for insurance? No. Insurance protects your interests as well. Your customer is still going to ask for their money back.

There is also another issue involved with insuring packages. Time & paperwork can be a big hassle; there is usually a lot more time and paperwork involved especially, if you ship with the Postal Service. In order for insurance to be valid, the proper form has to be filled out and "Ball Stamped" at the post office.

The only way to get a ball stamp is to stand in line the post office. This wastes valuable time. UPS has an easier method. Everything under $100 is automatically insured and there is not extra paper work. If insurance is very important to your business, you may want to consider only shipping with UPS. EBay transactions involve two types of insurance that might have an impact on your pocketbook:

Shipping insurance

This insurance covers your item as it travels through the U.S. Postal Service, UPS, FedEx, or any of the other carriers. Some well-informed sellers have signed up with a company called Package in- Transit Coverage, which insures all their packages through an annual policy. This way the seller does not have to stand in line at the post office to get the insurance stamp from the clerk. The seller logs the packages and reports on them about the shipped products on a monthly basis. Sellers will let you know that they use this service when they ship your item.

Fraud insurance

EBay's Fraud Protection Program provides some nominal insurance against fraud. EBay's Fraud Protection insurance pays up to $175 (a maximum of $200 minus a $25 deductible). Therefore, if you file a $50 claim, you get $25. If you file a $5,000 claim, you still only get $175. Remember that if you pay via PayPal, you may cover yourself for purchases up to $500.

Shipping

All those millions of items need to get from one place to another! Amazingly, eBay claims that between 5% -10% of all the packages shipped in the United States belong to their auction items.
Most auction items are shipped through one of three primary carriers i.e. the United States Postal Service *(USPS), United Parcel Service (UPS) and Federal Express (FedEx). Which* service is best for your needs, will depend on many factors. For small packages, Priority Mail is a safe, fast and cheap choice. For larger packages, you should get rate quotes from all three:

www.usps.gov
www.ups.com
www.fedex.com

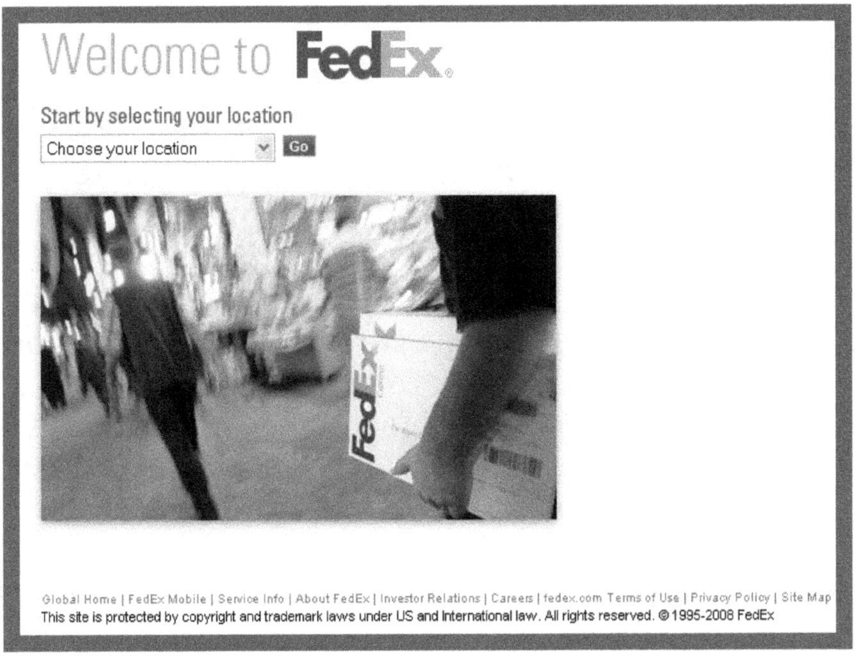

Large Items Shipping

New sellers often are intimidated when it comes to shipping very large items. How do you do it? Is it even worth it? Generally, the answer is no, if you only ship a large item every occasionally. The amount of time involved packing it correctly and finding the proper shipper may not be worth the time. Unless you are going to make a hefty profit, you may want to consider doing a "local pick-up" only. With that said, many eBay sellers make nice living selling huge items like appliances and couches.

You can ship items less than 40 lbs via UPS for a fair price, but over 40lbs and the price gets too expensive.

So, how do people ship large items? Freight delivery is the common shipping tool. Have you ever heard the term "FOB"? This means "Freight On Board". So if someone says, "Shipping is FOB Los Angeles, California" that means that you pay the shipping via a freight carrier to your location. Before we talk about freight carriers, let us discuss about packing. Most big items that are shipped via freight are "Crated". This means putting the products in a large wooden crate.

If you have a big eBay business, you can do this yourself. There are companies that will sell you the materials to do this. Some freight carriers will even crate your item for you, when they come to pick it up. Of course, it will cost you extra money. One such company that does this is:
http://www.transitsystems.com/

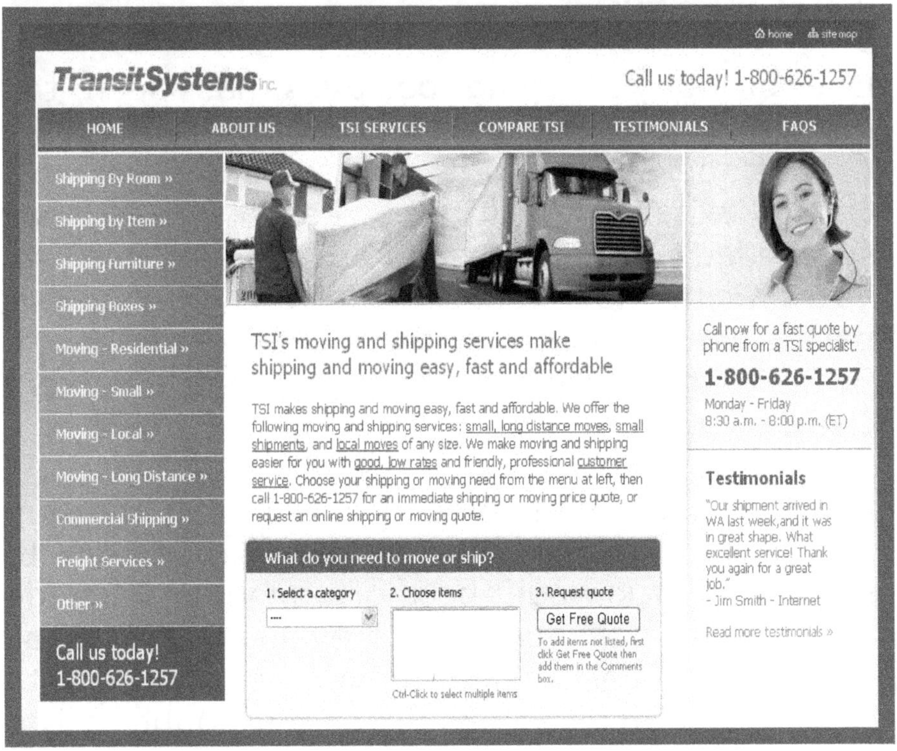

Many other companies offer a similar service. The best thing to do here is look in the Yellow Pages or do a search on the Internet for companies in your area that offer these services.

What is Feedback?

One of eBay's strong positives has been the formation of a well-knit community through its use of message boards, chats, and feedback. Many experts say the reason eBay has succeeded where dozens of other dot-com auction sites have failed is that eBay has always paid close attention to the needs of its users. Even in the early days, the concept was very clear.

Pierre and his employees figured that, if users complained openly (for all other members to see), feedback would be more genuine. The "do unto others" philosophy prevailed; above all else, Pierre encouraged buyers and sellers to give each other the benefit of the doubt and to conduct themselves professionally.

However, the *piece de resistance* of feedback policy, the part that makes eBay work, is the fact that Pierre and his staff encouraged users to give positive feedback, as long as they give negative or neutral feedback. The benefits of the feedback policy are immediately clear. Before even placing a bid with a seller, a buyer (you) can check the experience other eBay buyers have had doing business with a particular seller.

You can see whether items in a seller's previous auctions shipped quickly, whether they reached the buyer safely, whether communication was clear and frequent, and so on.

You now have more information about an eBay seller then you have, when you walk into a new store in your neighborhood! Every eBay member has a feedback rating. Buyers rate sellers, and sellers rate buyers — no one is immune. A seller might comment on how quickly you paid for an item, how well you communicated, or how you reacted to a problem.

There are three types of feedback:

- Neutral Feedback
- Positive Feedback
- Negative Feedback

Neutral feedback

You can leave neutral feedback, if you feel so-so about a specific transaction. It is the middle-of-the-road comment that is useful when, for example, you bought an item that has a little more wear and tear on it than the seller indicated, but you still like it and want to keep it with you.

Positive feedback

Someone once said, "All you have is your reputation." Reputation is what makes eBay function. If the transaction works well, you get positive feedback; whenever the situation warrants; you should give it right back.

Negative feedback

If there is a glitch or a problem with the product quality or shipment, you have the ultimate right — as someone would say *obligation* — to leave negative feedback.

Make Your Feedback Score

Here is the cool way to build your feedback ratings. Those are kind of like magical numbers, on which people start feeling extra comfortable. Just think of it from the buyer's viewpoint. The way to do that is getting your early feedback by buying, not selling. Here is what you do: you go to eBay and type in the word "e-book."

There are a lot of people selling knowledge products or e-books. An e-book is an electronic book. Seller will deliver it in a digital format, so they do not have to mail it to you. Type in "e-book;" press enter.

On the right-hand column, you will see those who have free shipping. What you want to do here is to find people who are selling an e-book for like 60, 70, or 80 cents with free shipping. Buying from them allows you collect positive feedback for less than a buck.

Of course, if there are items you need to get, go ahead and do that. You might need to buy labels, toner or ink for your printer, DVD blanks, and CD blanks. You are probably going to find it cheaper on eBay than Staples or Office Max. For building up your feedback quick, a great trick is to buy your way; buy e-books; buy information products because they are cheaper.

Your score can go up once per unique transaction. Feedback is positive, negative, or neutral. So, if you are focusing on building your feedback, make sure that you only buy one item from each unique person. Another way of helping your customer to trust you is by being a bonded seller through BuySafe. When looking at an item for sale on eBay, and you see the BuySafe insignia, it tells a potential buyer that they are protected for this transaction. Even if the seller goes bankrupt, the buyer cannot lose! The seller pays a very small fee for each bonded auction. The service does not cost the buyer a single penny! It can dramatically raise the selling price of auction items.

How can I Leave Feedback?

Several ways are available to leave feedback comments:

- If you are on the user's feedback page, click the *Leave Feedback* link; now, the *Leave Feedback* page appears.
- In the *All Buying — Won* or the *All Selling — Sold area* of your *My eBay* page, click the *Leave Feedback* link next to the auction.
- Go to your auction and click the *Leave Feedback* link. In the *Feedback Form*, click the *Leave Feedback* link to see a list of all your completed auctions from the last 90 days.
- Click the *Services* link, above the main navigation bar, and then click eBay *Feedback Form*. On the next page that appears, click the *Leave Feedback* link.

To leave feedback, enter the required information. Choose whether you want your feedback to be positive, negative, or neutral. Type your feedback comment and click the *Leave Feedback* button.

How can Deal with Negative Feedback?

Many eBay users are zealous and protective about their feedback ratings. Although it is a good thing to own a high rating, some users get over obsessive about it.

For that reason, you want to be very sure of yourself before you leave negative feedback about a user. Some overly zealous users might retaliate by leaving negative feedback about you, even if it looks inappropriate on your part. Unfortunately, there's not much you can do, if you receive negative feedback; under normal conditions, you cannot withdraw feedback comments.

There have been some exceptions, when the feedback has been obscene or slanderous in nature. What you can do is offer a response to the feedback, which you do by going to your Feedback page, then scrolling down to and clicking the *Reply to Feedback Received* link. When the feedback comments list appears, click the *Reply* link next to a particular comment and then enter your response. Your new comment will be below the original feedback comment on the *Feedback Profile* page. Just try not to get defensive; the best response is one that is calm, clear, and well reasoned.

Sell you Items for the Highest Price

Always put your item in the right category. There are shoppers who only shop by checking the category list repeatedly, limiting the number of possible buyers. Some people think that the most general category possible will get their item the most views, but this is not true on eBay. If you are listing sixteen items, take a few seconds to double check your listing details, so you do not put items in the wrong category.

Not researching the item you are selling is a common fault. Besides knowing what to call your item, you should research its inherent value. There could be six of the exact same item listed for $2.99 each, but your price is $12.00. It does not take a genius to see that your auction is the last of these auctions to get a cursory look, let alone a bid.

Take a good clear picture of your item, as close up as you can, to get the entire item into the picture. Before you click the shutter, see if there is anything ugly or unnecessary in the immediate background. You could move the background distraction or put your item in another location to take the picture. Later, you will need to edit and optimize your images. With the help of a photo-editing program, crop the picture to include the item only.

No one cares about your living room, and it is maddening to wait forever for a photo to load only to find out that your time was an utter waste, because the seller could not take a minute to crop his or her picture. Tweak the color of your item until it matches as much as possible.

Most collectors specialize, and the color does make a difference to them. Next, shrink your picture down to 72 dpi (which is the most that monitors see anyway) to make your picture load faster. If your starting picture is small, you can shrink the dpi without shrinking the size of the picture that people will see.

If your picture fills the entire screen, you can probably make it much smaller, so it loads faster and makes for quicker viewing. When you want to highlight a special zone in the images, make a copy of your large picture before shrinking it, and then crop out a "close-up" view of that feature only as a second photo.

Try sharpening your photo - sometimes this helps and sometimes sharpening makes the picture look worse, but you can always click on undo. When you take pictures without enough light, you will have many problems. The color will never come out correct, even with good photo editing software.

A white item will look dirty and gray, and lightening the picture does not help much either. In addition, shadows can look like flaws to buyers. It always makes for a better photo, if you adjust your camera to match the lighting you are using.

Be honest with your photos and images. You might put into your written description that the item has a "small" defect in the back. Showing a photo of the perfect side only would be deceptive on your part, and it makes many buyers not trust you.

If a buyer's idea of a small defect is much different from yours, you will end up with a very unhappy customer and possibly have to issue a refund to keep your reputation. You don't have to put a large close-up of the flaw, since this makes the problem look worse than it really is, but do show both sides of the item at the same size, if one side has a problem. Buyers may decide that the flaw is not enough to bother them. Reserve auctions can make both sides happier. The seller in an auction does not have to sell the item for less than $28.00; if the reserve price is $28.00, ($27.99 is even better). Nevertheless, if that seller makes the opening price $9.99, the buyers will still think DEAL even after seeing that there is a reserve. This brings competition without the risk or difficulties.

The most common reason for using a reserve is in case eBay has an outage, the buyers cannot get in and bid, and it is good insurance in a questionable economy.

Some sellers think that they can say about six words about an item since they put in a photo. No. People with older computers, on a bad ISP, or that just highly value their time do a lot of their shopping without photos.

They "turn off" the photos in their browser and search by written descriptions alone. At least, put a real description of what the item is. This is also highly valuable when people do extensive searches. A search cannot find a 3" Goofy in a karate outfit, if the description only says, "No damage, shipping is extra." Added to all of that is the title of "Goofy Toy," and you can see how difficult it would be for this item to be found.

Few Goofy collectors want to do a search for "goofy" just to find one special one - there are thousands of Goofy items listed, including Goofy Grape and someone who tells you he got the item from his goofy brother. Write your description in an effort to answer any question buyers might have. You could get many, many buyers looking during the last five minutes, and that simply not enough time to ask a question and get the answer.

Getting a question answered was much quicker before eBay made themselves the mediators. In fact, it is to your benefit to put your email address in your description for last-minute questions. Anyone, who ever goes anywhere on the internet will have their email address added to "spam" email lists.

It is just the price, which we pay for the privilege of talking to anyone in the world free (no stamp, no phone bill). Hitting the delete key is not hard to do. If you have kids and worry about the possibility of receiving adult-type email, do not let the kids use email until you check the mail. Anyway, if a buyer does not have enough time to get their questions answered, they will most likely not bid.

In the event that someone has a question in the last hour or two, or even the last 24 hours (when your item is in the "ending today" category), do your best to be available. Check your email often. The more people that find your auction through a search, the more bids you could get theoretically, depending on all other factors also. Include your item name in the description. Adding the color (although it seems obvious by the photo) may double your amount of visitors. People search in different ways, and they do not all spell the same or use the same terms.

For example, using "eye glasses," "eyeglasses" and "spectacles" in your description will bring in three times the number of visitors, as any one of these alone. Add the maker's name also, if you know it.

If you are new to selling, do a lot of browsing first. See how other auctions look. If you do not have a photo-editing program, you will need to find one, if you are going to list more than one auction.

"God Bless to all My Family & Friends. You are always in my prayers whether I tell you daily or not"

Harry J. Misner

FREE BONUS

Once my new website is finished being designed, everyone who purchases any of my books will be granted lifetime access to my Author Website:

http://www.harrymisner.com/

Here, you will be able to ask me any questions you might have via email and purchase updated or additional books of mine at a discounted rate.

Dedication: I dedicate this book to my beautiful son Collin, who just turned 3 years old this September and is currently battling Autism. I constantly call him my little Angel, because he has changed my life more than I have ever dreamed or imagined possible.

I love you friend!

"Today, 1 in 150 individuals are diagnosed with autism, making it more common than pediatric cancer, diabetes, and AIDS combined."

So please help the fight, visit
http://www.autismspeaks.org/

The Top Google Searches for the terms "eBay", "Make Money from Home", and "Home Based Business"

100 Home Based Business, A Home Based Business Online, Adult Home Based Business, Amazing Home Based Business, And Make Money From Home, Arise Home Based Business, At Home Based Business, At Home Business, At Home Job, Auction Sites, Best Home Based Business, Best Way To Make Money From Home, Best Ways To Make Money, Better Than Ebay, Boats On Ebay, Books On Ebay, Business Earn From Home Money, Business Idea, Business Ideas, Business Opportunities, Business Opportunity, Business Start Up, Business Startup, Buy And Sell On Ebay, Buy Ebay, Buy On Ebay, Can I Make Money Working From Home, Can You Really Make Money From Home, Car Auction, Cgi.ebay, Christian Home Based Business, Computer Home Based Business, Data Entry, Data Entry At Home, Data Entry From Home, Data Entry Job, Data Entry Jobs, Data Entry Work, Dildos On Ebay, Dropshippers, Dropshipping, E Bay Com, E-bay, Eaby, Eaby Com, Earn At Home, Earn Cash At Home, Earn Cash From Home, Earn Extra Cash, Earn Extra Income, Earn Extra Money, Earn From Home, Earn Money, Earn Money At Home, Earn Money From Home, Earn Money On The Internet, Earn Money Online, Earning Money, Easiest Home Based Business, Easy Home Based Business, Easy Money, Easy Money From Home, Easy Ways To Make Money, Eba, Ebay, Ebay $1, Ebay Account, Ebay Adult, Ebay Au, Ebay Auction, Ebay Auction Uk, Ebay Auctions, Ebay Aus, Ebay Aust, Ebay Australia, Ebay Auto, Ebay Auto Parts, Ebay Automobiles, Ebay Bakugan, Ebay Bikes, Ebay Book, Ebay Business, Ebay C Om, Ebay COm, Ebay Ca, Ebay Canada, Ebay Car, Ebay Cars For Sale, Ebay Cim, Ebay Classified, Ebay Classifieds, Ebay Co M, Ebay Co Uk, Ebay Co.uk, Ebay Co0m, Ebay Coj, Ebay Cojm, Ebay Com, Ebay Com Au, Ebay Computers, Ebay Contact Number, Ebay Coupon, Ebay Cpom, Ebay Credit, Ebay Credit Card, Ebay Disney, Ebay Dvd, Ebay Ebay, Ebay Find, Ebay For Dummies, Ebay Free Shipping, Ebay Garmin, Ebay Harley Davidson, Ebay Home Page, Ebay Homepage, Ebay India, Ebay Ireland, Ebay Lcom, Ebay Local, Ebay M, Ebay Marketing, Ebay Mastercard, Ebay Motor, Ebay Motorcycle, Ebay Motors, Ebay Motors Motorcycles, Ebay Motors Uk, Ebay Music, Ebay Net, Ebay Official Site, Ebay Online, Ebay Promotional Codes, Ebay Psp, Ebay Register, Ebay Registration, Ebay Selling, Ebay Shop, Ebay Shopping, Ebay Sign Up, Ebay Singapore, Ebay Site, Ebay Software, Ebay Store, Ebay Store Locations, Ebay Stores, Ebay Suspension, Ebay Templates, Ebay Textbooks, Ebay Tools, Ebay Travel, Ebay Tv, Ebay Uk, Ebay Uk Com, Ebay Usa, Ebay Used Cars, Ebay Vom, Ebay Wanted, Ebay Web, Ebay Web Site, Ebay Website, Ebay Wedding, Ebay World, Ebay Xbox, Ebay.au, Ebay.c, Ebay.ca, Ebay.co.uk, Ebay.com, Ebay.com.au, Ebay.in, Ebays, Ebby, Ebey, Eby, Eby Com, Eebay, Ernstings, Extra Income, Extra Income Idea, Extra Money, Extra Money From Home, Fast Money, Free Home Based Business, Free Home Based Business Opportunity, Freedom Home Based Business, From Home Based Business, From Home Make Money Opportunity, From Home To Make Extra Money, Fun Home Based Business, Golf Carts For Sale On Ebay, Google Com, Google Ebay, Google Make Money From Home, Great Home Based Business, Green Home Based Business, Guitars On Ebay, Home Base Business, Home Based Business, Home Based Business Advertising, Home Based Business Advice, Home Based Business Article, Home Based Business Association, Home Based Business Books, Home Based Business Canada, Home Based Business Club, Home Based Business Com, Home Based Business Companies.

Home Based Business Connection, Home Based Business Consulting, Home Based Business Data, Home Based Business Earn, Home Based Business Entrepreneur, Home Based Business Entrepreneurs, Home Based Business Forum, Home Based Business Guide, Home Based Business Health, Home Based Business Idea, Home Based Business In Canada, Home Based Business Income, Home Based Business Info, Home Based Business Information, Home Based Business Insurance, Home Based Business Jobs, Home Based Business List, Home Based Business Office, Home Based Business Opportunities, Home Based Business Opportunities Online, Home Based Business Opportunity Seeker, Home Based Business Org, Home Based Business Owners, Home Based Business Plan, Home Based Business Program, Home Based Business Resources, Home Based Business Scam, Home Based Business Scams, Home Based Business Selling, Home Based Business Series, Home Based Business Show, Home Based Business Shows, Home Based Business Sites, Home Based Business Software, Home Based Business Start Up, Home Based Business Startup, Home Based Business Success, Home Based Business System, Home Based Business Systems, Home Based Business Tax, Home Based Business That, Home Based Business That Works, Home Based Business To Start, Home Based Business Usa, Home Based Business Web, Home Based Business Website, Home Based Business With, Home Based Business Work, Home Based Business World, Home Based Businesses, Home Based Bussiness, Home Based Entrepreneur, Home Based Entrepreneurs, Home Based Franchise Business, Home Based Job, Home Based Jobs, Home Based Marketing Business, Home Based Network Marketing Business, Home Based Retail Business, Home Based Sales Business, Home Based Small Business, Home Based Small Businesses, Home Based Work, Home Business, Home Employment, Home Job, Home Jobs, Home Typist, Home Work, Home-based Business, Home-based Business Opportunity, Home-based Businesses, Homebased, Homebased Business, Hotmail Com, How Can You Make Money From Home, How Make Money From Home, How To Earn Extra Income, How To Earn Money, How To Make Easy Money, How To Make Extra Money, How To Make Extra Money From Home, How To Make Extra Money Working From Home, How To Make Fast Money, How To Make Money, How To Make Money At Home, How To Make Money From Home, How To Make Money From Home For Free, How To Make Money From Home Free, How To Make Money From Home Legitimately, How To Make Money From Home No Scams, How To Make Money On The Internet, How To Make Money Online, How To Make Money Working From Home, How To Make More Money From Home, How To Make Quick Money, How To Sell On Ebay, How To Start A Business, How To Start A Home Based Business, How To Start A New Business, How To Start A Small Business, How To Start Home Based Business, How To Start Your Own Business, How To Use Ebay, How To Work From Home, Hse24, Http Www Ebay Com, I Make Money From Home, I Need To Make Money From Home, I Want A Home Based Business, I Want To Make Money, I Want To Make Money From Home, Ideas For A Home Based Business, Ideas For Home Based Business, Ideas Home Based Business, Ideas On How To Make Money From Home, Ideas To Make Money From Home, International Home Based Business, Internet Home Based Business, Internet Income, Internet Money, Internet Money Making, Is It Possible To Make Money From Home, Jobs From Home, Join Ebay, Jpc, Laptops On Ebay, Latest Home Based Business, Legitimate Home Based Business, Legitimate Home Based Businesses.

Legitimate Make Money From, Legitmate Home Based Business, Like Ebay, List Of Home Based Business, Made Money From Home, Make Cash From Home, Make Easy Money From Home, Make Extra Money, Make Extra Money From Home, Make Lots Of Money From Home, Make Lots Of Money Working From Home, Make Money, Make Money At Home, Make Money By Working From Home, Make Money Easy, Make Money Fast, Make Money Fast From Home, Make Money Free From Home, Make Money From Home, Make Money From Home As, Make Money From Home At, Make Money From Home Blog, Make Money From Home Business, Make Money From Home By, Make Money From Home Com, Make Money From Home Computer, Make Money From Home For, Make Money From Home For Free, Make Money From Home Forum, Make Money From Home Ideas, Make Money From Home In, Make Money From Home Internet, Make Money From Home Jobs, Make Money From Home Legitimate, Make Money From Home Legitimately, Make Money From Home Making, Make Money From Home No, Make Money From Home No Investment, Make Money From Home No Scam, Make Money From Home No Scams, Make Money From Home Not, Make Money From Home Now, Make Money From Home On, Make Money From Home On The, Make Money From Home On The Internet, Make Money From Home Part, Make Money From Home Review, Make Money From Home Reviews, Make Money From Home Scam, Make Money From Home Scams, Make Money From Home Selling, Make Money From Home System, Make Money From Home That, Make Money From Home Today, Make Money From Home Typing, Make Money From Home Using, Make Money From Home With, Make Money From Home Without, Make Money From Home Without Paying, Make Money From Home Writing, Make Money From Work, Make Money Internet, Make Money Now, Make Money On Ebay, Make Money On Internet, Make Money On The Internet, Make Money Online, Make Money Online From Home, Make Money Over The Internet, Make Money Today, Make Money With No Money, Make Money Working From Home, Make More Money From Home, Make Quick Money, Make Quick Money From Home, Make Real Money From Home, Make Real Money Working From Home, Making Cash From Home, Making Money, Making Money At Home, Making Money Easy, Making Money From Home, Making Money On Ebay, Making Money On The Internet, Making Money On The Web, Mlm Home Based Business, Money, Money At Home, Money From Home, Money Home Based Business, Money Making Ideas, Money Making Opportunities, Money Making Opportunity, My Ebay, My Ebay Account, My Ebay Sign In, My Home Based Business, New Business, New Business Ideas, New Home Based Business, Newest Home Based Business, Online Business Ideas, Online Business Opportunities, Online Data Entry, Online Data Entry Job, Online Data Entry Jobs, Online Home Based Business, Online Money, Online Money Making, Online Work, Own Business, Own Home Based Business, Oztion, Part Time Work From Home, Popular Home Based Business, Professional Home Based Business, Profitable Home Based Business, Prosperous Home Based Business, Ps2 Ebay, Purses Ebay, Quick Money, Quick Money Making, Real Ways To Make Money From Home, Really Make Money From Home, Really Make Money Working From Home, Reliable Home Based Business, Reputable Home Based Business, Residual Income, Sarah Palin Ebay, Search Ebay, Sell Items On Ebay, Sell On Ebay, Sell Stuff On Ebay, Selling On Ebay, Service Home Based Business, Setting Up A Home Based Business, Shoes On Ebay, Shop.ebay.com.

Similar To Ebay, Simple Home Based Business, Small Business, Small Business Idea, Small Business Ideas, Small Businesses, Start A Business, Start A Home Based Business, Start A Home Based Business On The Internet, Start A Small Business, Start Business, Start Home Based Business, Start My Own Home Based Business, Start Your Own Business, Starting A Business, Starting A Home Based Business, Starting A New Business, Starting A Small Business, Starting A Small Home Based Business, Starting An Online Business, Starting Business, Starting Home Based Business, Starting Your Own Business, Starting Your Own Home Based Business, Stuff To Sell On Ebay, Successful Business, Successful Home Based Business, The Best Way To Make Money From Home, The Home Based Business, To Make Money At Home, To Make Money From Home, To Make Money Working From Home, Top 10 Home Based Business, Tractors For Sale On Ebay, Tractors On Ebay, True Home Based Business, Want To Make Money From Home, Ways To Make Extra Money, Ways To Make Money, Ways To Make Money From Home, Ways To Make Money Working From Home, We Sell Your Stuff On Ebay, What Can I Do From Home To Make Money, What Is The Best Way To Make Money From Home, Wholesale Dropshippers, Wii On Ebay, Womens Home Based Business, Work At Home, Work At Home Business, Work At Home Internet, Work At Home Job, Work At Home Mom, Work At Home Moms, Work At Home Opportunities, Work From Home, Work From Home Business, Work From Home Jobs, Work From Home Opportunities, Workathome, Working At Home, Working From Home, Ww.ebay, Www Eaby Com, Www Eba, Www Ebay, Www Ebay C Om, Www Ebay Ca, Www Ebay Ccom, Www Ebay Cm, Www Ebay Co M, Www Ebay Co Uk, Www Ebay Coim, Www Ebay Coj, Www Ebay Cojm, Www Ebay Com, Www Ebay Com Au, Www Ebay Com Usa, Www Ebay Comm, Www Ebay Coom, Www Ebay Copm, Www Ebay Cpm, Www Ebay Om, Www Ebay Uk, Www Ebay Xom, Www Home Based Business, Www.ebay, Www.ebay. Uk, Www.ebay.c, Www.ebay.ca, Www.ebay.co, Www.ebay.co.uk, Www.ebay.com, Www.ebay.com.au, Wwwebay, Xbox 360 Ebay, You Can Make Money From Home, You Make Money From Home.

The common misspellings of the terms "eBay", "Make Money from Home", and "Home Based Business"

Ebay, Bay, Eay, Eby, Eba, Beay, Eaby, Ebya, Eebay, Ebbay, Ebaay, Ebayy, Wbay, Rbay, Evay, Enay, Ebsy, Ebat, Ebau, 3bay, 4bay, Dbay, Sbay, Egay, Ehay, Ebqy, Ebwy, Ebzy, Eba6, Eba7, Ebah, Ebag, Make Money From Home, Makemoney From Home, Make Moneyfrom Home, Make Money Fromhome, Makemoneyfrom Home, Makemoney Fromhome, Make Moneyfromhome, Makemoneyfromhome, Make Money Home From, Make From Money Home, Make From Home Money, Make Home Money From, Make Home From Money, Money Make From Home, Money Make Home From, Money From Make Home, Money From Home Make, Money Home Make From, Money Home From Make, From Make Money Home, From Make Home Money, From Money Make Home, From Money Home Make, From Home Make Money, From Home Money Make, Home Make Money From, Home Make From Money, Home Money Make From, Home Money From Make.

Home From Make Money, Home From Money Make, Ake Money From Home, Mke Money From Home, Mae Money From Home, Mak Money From Home, Make Oney From Home, Make Mney From Home, Make Moey From Home, Make Mony From Home, Make Mone From Home, Make Money Rom Home. Make Money Fom Home, Make Money Frm Home, Make Money Fro Home, Make Money From Ome, Make Money From Hme, Make Money From Hoe, Make Money From Hom, Amke Money From Home, Mkae Money From Home, Maek Money From Home, Make Omney From Home, Make Mnoey From Home, Make Moeny From Home, Make Monye From Home, Make Money Rfom Home, Make Money Form Home, Make Money Frmo Home, Make Money From Ohme, Make Money From Hmoe, Make Money From Hoem, Mmake Money From Home, Maake Money From Home, Makke Money From Home, Makee Money From Home, Make Mmoney From Home, Make Mooney From Home, Make Monney From Home, Make Moneey From Home, Make Moneyy From Home, Make Money Ffrom Home, Make Money Frrom Home, Make Money Froom Home, Make Money Fromm Home, Make Money From Hhome, Make Money From Hoome, Make Money From Homme, Make Money From Homee, Nake Money From Home, ,ake Money From Home, Mske Money From Home, Maje Money From Home, Male Money From Home, Makw Money From Home, Makr Money From Home, Make Noney From Home, Make ,oney From Home, Make Miney From Home, Make Mpney From Home, Make Mobey From Home, Make Momey From Home, Make Monwy From Home, Make Monry From Home, Make Monet From Home, Make Moneu From Home, Make Money Drom Home, Make Money Grom Home, Make Money Feom Home, Make Money Ftom Home, Make Money Frim Home, Make Money Frpm Home, Make Money Fron Home, Make Money Fro, Home, Make Money From Gome, Make Money From Jome, Make Money From Hime, Make Money From Hpme, Make Money From Hone, Make Money From Ho,e, Make Money From Homw, Make Money From Homr, Jake Money From Home, Kake Money From Home, Mqke Money From Home, Mwke Money From Home, Mzke Money From Home, Maie Money From Home, Maoe Money From Home, Ma,e Money From Home, Mame Money From Home, Mak3 Money From Home, Mak4 Money From Home, Makd Money From Home, Maks Money From Home, Make Joney From Home, Make Koney From Home, Make M9ney From Home, Make M0ney From Home, Make Mlney From Home, Make Mkney From Home, Make Mohey From Home, Make Mojey From Home, Make Mon3y From Home, Make Mon4y From Home, Make Mondy From Home, Make Monsy From Home, Make Mone6 From Home, Make Mone7 From Home, Make Moneh From Home, Make Moneg From Home, Make Money Rrom Home, Make Money Trom Home, Make Money Vrom Home, Make Money Crom Home, Make Money F4om Home, Make Money F5om Home, Make Money Ffom Home.

Make Money Fdom Home, Make Money Fr9m Home, Make Money Fr0m Home, Make Money Frlm Home, Make Money Frkm Home, Make Money Froj Home, Make Money Frok Home, Make Money From Yome, Make Money From Uome, Make Money From Nome, Make Money From Bome, Make Money From H9me, Make Money From H0me, Make Money From Hlme, Make Money From Hkme, Make Money From Hoje, Make Money From Hoke, Make Money From Hom3, Make Money From Hom4, Make Money From Homd, Make Money From Homs, Home Based Business, Homebased Business, Home Basedbusiness, Homebasedbusiness, Home Business Based, Based Home Business, Based Business Home, Business Home Based, Business Based Home, Ome Based Business, Hme Based Business, Hoe Based Business, Hom Based Business, Home Ased Business, Home Bsed Business, Home Baed Business, Home Basd Business, Home Base Business, Home Based Usiness, Home Based Bsiness, Home Based Buiness. Home Based Busness, Home Based Busiess, Home Based Businss, Home Based Busines, Ohme Based Business, Hmoe Based Business, Hoem Based Business, Home Absed Business, Home Bsaed Business, Home Baesd Business, Home Basde Business, Home Based Ubsiness, Home Based Bsuiness, Home Based Buisness, Home Based Busniess, Home Based Busienss, Home Based Businses, Hhome Based Business, Hoome Based Business, Homme Based Business, Homee Based Business, Home Bbased Business, Home Baased Business, Home Bassed Business, Home Baseed Business, Home Basedd Business, Home Based Bbusiness, Home Based Buusiness, Home Based Bussiness, Home Based Busiiness, Home Based Businness, Home Based Busineess, Home Based Businesss, Gome Based Business, Jome Based Business, Hime Based Business, Hpme Based Business, Hone Based Business, Ho,e Based Business, Homw Based Business, Homr Based Business, Home Vased Business, Home Nased Business, Home Bssed Business, Home Baaed Business, Home Baded Business, Home Baswd Business, Home Basrd Business, Home Bases Business, Home Basef Business, Home Based Vusiness, Home Based Nusiness, Home Based Bysiness, Home Based Bisiness, Home Based Buainess, Home Based Budiness, Home Based Busuness, Home Based Busoness, Home Based Busibess, Home Based Busimess, Home Based Businwss, Home Based Businrss, Home Based Busineas, Home Based Busineds, Home Based Businesa, Home Based Businesd, Yome Based Business, Uome Based Business, Nome Based Business, Bome Based Business, H9me Based Business, H0me Based Business, Hlme Based Business, Hkme Based Business, Hoje Based Business, Hoke Based Business, Hom3 Based Business, Hom4 Based Business, Homd Based Business, Homs Based Business, Home Gased Business, Home Hased Business, Home Bqsed Business, Home Bwsed Business, Home Bzsed Business, Home Bawed Business, Home Baeed Business, Home Baxed Business, Home Bazed Business, Home Bas3d Business, Home Bas4d Business, Home Basdd Business.

Home Bassd Business, Home Basee Business, Home Baser Business, Home Basec Business, Home Basex Business, Home Based Gusiness, Home Based Husiness, Home Based B7siness, Home Based B8siness, Home Based Bjsiness, Home Based Bhsiness, Home Based Buwiness, Home Based Bueiness, Home Based Buxiness, Home Based Buziness, Home Based Bus8ness, Home Based Bus9ness, Home Based Buskness, Home Based Busjness, Home Based Busihess, Home Based Busijess, Home Based Busin3ss, Home Based Busin4ss, Home Based Busindss, Home Based Businsss, Home Based Businews, Home Based Businees, Home Based Businexs, Home Based Businezs, Home Based Businesw, Home Based Businese, Home Based Businesx, Home Based Businesz.

- Business & Economics
- Business / Economics / Finance
- Business/Economics
- Business & Economics / E-Commerce / Internet Marketing
- Business & Economics : E-Commerce - Online Trading
- Business & Economics : Industries - Retailing
- E-Commerce - Internet Marketing
- E-Commerce - Online Trading
- Industries - Retailing

Books > Computers & Internet > Business & Culture > **eBay**
Books > Business & Investing > Industries & Professions > E-commerce > **Online Trading**
Books > Business & Investing > Industries & Professions > **Retailing**

www.ingramcontent.com/pod-product-compliance
Lightning Source LLC
Chambersburg PA
CBHW051521170526
45165CB00002B/551
9781440442506